Acting Edition

Curiosities

Short Plays

by Steve Yockey

Adorable Kitten Image Collapse
Cough Syrup
Dark Suburban Still Life with Small Figure
Everything That Happened Before That Terrible Holiday Sweater Party
Fluff
Go Get 'em, Tiger!
Good Luck Fortune Cookies
I Buried Doug Biggers Alive but He's Probably Dead by Now
Music for an Abandoned Zoo
A Mysterious Horse
She Said Everything's Moving Faster
Telephones & Bad Weather
Vacuum
© 2025 by Steve Yockey
All Rights Reserved

CURIOSITIES is fully protected under the copyright laws of the United States of America, the British Commonwealth, including Canada, and all member countries of the Berne Convention for the Protection of Literary and Artistic Works, the Universal Copyright Convention, and/or the World Trade Organization conforming to the Agreement on Trade Related Aspects of Intellectual Property Rights. All rights, including professional and amateur stage productions, recitation, lecturing, public reading, motion picture, radio broadcasting, television, online/digital production, and the rights of translation into foreign languages are strictly reserved.

ISBN 978-0-573-71159-6

www.concordtheatricals.com
www.concordtheatricals.co.uk

FOR PRODUCTION INQUIRIES

UNITED STATES AND CANADA
info@concordtheatricals.com
1-866-979-0447

UNITED KINGDOM AND EUROPE
licensing@concordtheatricals.co.uk
020-7054-7298

Each title is subject to availability from Concord Theatricals Corp., depending upon country of performance. Please be aware that *CURIOSITIES* may not be licensed by Concord Theatricals Corp. in your territory. Professional and amateur producers should contact the nearest Concord Theatricals Corp. office or licensing partner to verify availability.

CAUTION: Professional and amateur producers are hereby warned that *CURIOSITIES* is subject to a licensing fee. The purchase, renting, lending or use of this book does not constitute a license to perform this title(s), which license must be obtained from Concord Theatricals Corp. prior to any performance. Performance of this title(s) without a license is a violation of federal law and may subject the producer and/or presenter of such performances to civil penalties. Both amateurs and professionals considering a production are strongly advised to apply to the appropriate agent before starting rehearsals, advertising, or booking a theatre. A licensing fee must be paid whether the title(s) is presented for charity or gain and whether or not admission is charged. Professional/Stock licensing fees are quoted upon application to Concord Theatricals Corp.

This work is published by Samuel French, an imprint of Concord Theatricals Corp.

No one shall make any changes in this title(s) for the purpose of production. No part of this book may be reproduced, stored in a retrieval system, scanned, uploaded, or transmitted in any form, by any means, now known or yet to be invented, including mechanical, electronic, digital, photocopying, recording, videotaping, or otherwise, without the prior written permission of the publisher. No one shall share this title(s), or any part of this title(s), through any social media or file hosting websites.

For all inquiries regarding motion picture, television, online/digital and other media rights, please contact Concord Theatricals Corp.

MUSIC AND THIRD-PARTY MATERIALS USE NOTE

Licensees are solely responsible for obtaining formal written permission from copyright owners to use copyrighted music and/or other copyrighted third-party materials (e.g. artworks, logos) in the performance of this play and are strongly cautioned to do so. If no such permission is obtained by the licensee, then the licensee must use only original music and materials that the licensee owns and controls. Licensees are solely responsible and liable for clearances of all third-party copyrighted materials, including without limitation music, and shall indemnify the copyright owners of the play(s) and their licensing agent, Concord Theatricals Corp., against any costs, expenses, losses and liabilities arising from the use of such copyrighted third-party materials by licensees. For music, please contact the appropriate music licensing authority in your territory for the rights to any incidental music.

IMPORTANT BILLING AND CREDIT REQUIREMENTS

If you have obtained performance rights to this title, please refer to your licensing agreement for important billing and credit requirements.

TABLE OF CONTENTS

Adorable Kitten Image Collapse 1

Cough Syrup 17

Dark Suburban Still Life with Small Figure 25

*Everything That Happened Before That Terrible Holiday
    Sweater Party* 39

Fluff 53

Go Get 'em, Tiger! 65

Good Luck Fortune Cookies 79

*I Buried Doug Biggers Alive but He's Probably
    Dead by Now* 93

Music for an Abandoned Zoo 109

A Mysterious Horse 119

She Said Everything's Moving Faster 127

Telephones & Bad Weather 135

Vacuum 151

Adorable Kitten Image Collapse

ADORABLE KITTEN IMAGE COLLAPSE premiered on June 1, 2017, as a part of the 22nd Summer Shorts Festival at Carnival Studio Theatre, Adrienne Arsht Center for the Performing Arts. It was commissioned by City Theatre (Margaret M. Ledford, Artistic Director) in Miami, FL. The production was directed by Paul Tei. The cast was as follows:

ANN MARIE . . . . Irene Adjan
RICK . . . . Brian Reiff
RICK'S LIZARD BRAIN . . . . Phillip Andrew Santiago
RICK'S CONSCIENCE . . . . Robert Strain
INTERNET GOD (1) . . . . Thiana Berrick
INTERNET GOD (2) . . . . Cassandra Zepeda

CHARACTERS

ANN MARIE – a woman, fond of posting cat photos

RICK – a man, an unrepentant Internet troll

RICK'S LIZARD BRAIN – Rick's seriously cocksure lizard brain

RICK'S CONSCIENCE – Rick's seriously malnourished conscience

INTERNET GOD (1) – one half of a technological deity appearing as two women

INTERNET GOD (2) – the other half of a technological deity appearing as two women

AUTHOR'S NOTES

[ ] in the script indicate overlapping dialogue.

This all moves quickly. It's fast and fun. It's not thoughtful.

The kitten projections should be as massive as possible and increasingly more adorable as the play progresses.

RICK'S LIZARD BRAIN and **RICK'S CONSCIENCE** might carry small signs that identify them for the duration of the play.

Portions of the **INTERNET GODS**' dialogue in quotation marks are spoken through an electronic megaphone.

NOTE ON IMAGE PROJECTIONS

A license to produce *Adorable Kitten Image Collapse* does not include a license to publicly display any third-party or copyrighted images. Licensees must acquire rights for any copyrighted images or create their own.

(**RICK** *is sitting at his kitchen table eating cereal. His laptop is open on the table and he scrolls through things, snickering to himself.*)

(**ANN MARIE** *walks onto stage. She's on the sidewalk outside Rick's place. She's carrying a large purse. She's clearly been crying, but not anymore. She pulls out a phone and hums a little tune to herself as she dials.**)

(**RICK**'s *phone vibrates. He picks it up and answers.*)

RICK. Yeah, what?

ANN MARIE. Oh! Oh my God, hi. Is this Rick? Oh my God, you answered.

RICK. Who the fuck is this?

ANN MARIE. Hey, Rick. This is Ann Marie Adams. @AnnMarieKittens from Twitter? You've been trolling me online?

(*A giant image of an adorable kitten appears above the set.*)

RICK. No way.

ANN MARIE. Yes way.

RICK. Wow! You're actually fucking calling me? You dumb bitch.

---

* A license to produce *Adorable Kitten Image Collapse* does not include a performance license for any third-party or copyrighted music. Licensees should create an original composition or use music in the public domain. For further information, please see the Music and Third-Party Materials Use Note on page iii.

ANN MARIE. Oh my god, it really is you. Great, this is so great!

RICK. What the fuck do you want?

ANN MARIE. Well, my friend is really good with, I don't know, computer stuff and after you tweeted that I'm a whore bitch seventy-two times in an hour and typed that you were going to "skull fuck me to death," he helped me find you.

RICK. Are you fucking crazy?

ANN MARIE. Maybe? I did have a nervous breakdown because of all your bullying. But I'm also definitely a real person with real feelings.

RICK. No, you are a sappy bitch who posts dumb fucking cat photos.

ANN MARIE. They make me happy. They make my girlfriend happy. Or they did until the nervous breakdown I mentioned.

RICK. How the hell did you have a girlfriend?

ANN MARIE. So back to the kittens, I'd argue that they at least can make people happy.

RICK. Fuck that, not me. And this is America so we have, ya know, freedom of speech. So I can say whatever the fuck I want.

ANN MARIE. Absolutely! We have freedom of speech, yes. And we also have, like, freedom of consequences. Like when people boycott things or protest one and other's free speech, right? So I'll see you outside.

RICK. Right, okay, like you're outside my place.

ANN MARIE. Yep. I have nothing else in my life now, so I'm going to hide in the dark, wait until you're not looking, stab you to death, go to jail forever, and then post cat pictures from prison. Because consequences.

(He looks down. She looks up, produces a large knife from her purse, and waves with a chipper smile.)

RICK. Holy fuck! You have a knife. You have a big, they were just words!

(A new and even more adorable kitten image appears.)

ANN MARIE. Oh, I know. I'm just saying words, too. Until I slit your throat. Okay bye!

(She smiles and hangs up. He starts hyperventilating.)

RICK. Holy fuck. Okay. Okay, okay, you guys?! You guys, get in here!

*(Two **MEN** enter in a rush. Well, **RICK'S LIZARD BRAIN** enters in a rush and **RICK'S CONSCIENCE** weakly stumbles in behind him. **RICK'S LIZARD BRAIN** is barefoot in shorts, a Hawaiian shirt, and cheap-looking neon frame sunglasses. **RICK'S CONSCIENCE** is wearing sneakers, jeans, and a tight T-shirt with a cartoon cricket emblazoned on it. His hands are bound together and he is wearing a gag.)*

RICK'S LIZARD BRAIN. What the fuck? Is it a fire? Is it a hot chick? What's going [on, man?]

RICK. [Shut-up!]

RICK'S LIZARD BRAIN. Whoa!

RICK. We are going to have a meeting, an emergency meeting, right now.

RICK'S LIZARD BRAIN. Is it about how you need to fucking chill this harsh vibe before you get dickslapped?

*(He laughs at his own joke and turns to get a high five from **RICK'S CONSCIENCE**, but that can't happen because of his bound hands. When he turns back, disappointed, **RICK** slaps him in the face.)*

RICK'S LIZARD BRAIN. What? The? Fuck?

RICK. I told you to shut up. Now listen, both of you. You are my lizard brain and you are my conscience and I think this is going to take all three of us. Got it? So there is a chick outside with a big knife and she wants to kill us.

RICK'S LIZARD BRAIN. Fuck you.

RICK. No, fuck you. She's right out there.

*(All three of them look. **ANN MARIE** waves excitedly with her big knife. All three of them jerk back out of view.)*

RICK'S LIZARD BRAIN. Holy shit!

RICK. I told you.

*(**RICK'S CONSCIENCE** struggles to speak. **RICK** yanks off his gag. Meanwhile, a new and even more adorable kitten image appears.)*

RICK'S CONSCIENCE. You guys, stop swearing so much. Also, are you going to finish that cereal? Because I am literally starving to [death over here.]

RICK'S LIZARD BRAIN. [How the fuck] [is that helping?]

RICK. [What is wrong] with you?

RICK'S CONSCIENCE. I'm your conscience and you've had me gagged and tied up under your bed since you were fourteen. I'm hungry, desperate, and pretty dizzy.

RICK. That's a really fucking terrible attitude, man.

RICK'S LIZARD BRAIN. Put the gag back in and let him starve to death.

RICK. That is also a really fucking terrible attitude, man.

RICK'S CONSCIENCE. Language. Okay, look. Let me try to, just, what did you do to her?

RICK. I didn't do anything! I like barely [did anything.]

RICK'S LIZARD BRAIN. [He didn't do] anything she didn't deserve.

RICK'S CONSCIENCE. I'm gonna pass out soon, so please just tell me what you did?

RICK. I mean I guess I said some mean shit to her because she kept posting these fucking annoying photos of kittens online [all the time.]

RICK'S LIZARD BRAIN. [Holy shit, those] fucking kittens. The worst.

RICK'S CONSCIENCE. And even though that doesn't have anything to do with you or effect you in any way, you attacked her [and caused her to...?]

RICK. [Whoa, whoa! Let's] back up on that "attack" thing. Sticks and stones, right? Words, right? I called her some names because she was annoying.

RICK'S LIZARD BRAIN. And you said you would skull fuck her to death. Yeah!

(They both look at him and he calms down.)

RICK'S CONSCIENCE. You guys, did you try apologizing?

RICK'S LIZARD BRAIN. [Fuck that! What is wrong with you?]

RICK. [I'm not apologizing to some chick.]

RICK'S CONSCIENCE. Well, that's all I've got. Good luck. Can I have some cereal now?

RICK. Fuck!

(Frustrated, **RICK** *hands a spoon to him.* **RICK'S CONSCIENCE** *sits down and starts wolfing down the cereal with his hands still tied together.)*

RICK'S LIZARD BRAIN. What if we just get high?

RICK. How does that fix this?

RICK'S LIZARD BRAIN. I just want to get high and play [World of Warcraft.]

RICK. [This is your fucking] fault because I let you run the [show online!]

RICK'S LIZARD BRAIN. [My fault?! Since] when the fuck am I the boss of you?!

*(***ANN MARIE*** pulls out her phone and starts dialing.)*

RICK'S CONSCIENCE. He's right. He's a terrible influence, [but he's right.]

RICK. [So help me, I] will take that cereal away from you and [throw it away.]

RICK'S CONSCIENCE. [Please don't take] away my cereal!

*(***RICK****'s phone vibrates again. He answers.)*

RICK. What?!

ANN MARIE. Hi! Sorry, it's me again. Still out here. I could hear you yelling and I just wanted to say that this is definitely all your fault. By the way, if you call the police I'll just leave and come back later. Also, they'll probably take you in on the outstanding bench warrant for unpaid parking tickets that my friend found while tracking you down for me. Did you get those from leaving your car street parked because you don't go out very much? Anyway, kill you soon, okay bye.

(She hangs up. A new and even more adorable kitten image appears.)

RICK. Hello? Hello?!

RICK'S CONSCIENCE. I think she hung up.

RICK. You think?!

RICK'S LIZARD BRAIN. I can't believe that bitch [hung up on us.]

RICK. [I think she's] really going [to kill me.]

RICK'S CONSCIENCE. [You guys, this] cereal is delicious.

*(**RICK** knocks the bowl of cereal out of his hands and onto the floor. **RICK'S CONSCIENCE** just takes it in with a kind of pitiful shock.)*

RICK'S LIZARD BRAIN. I know what to do! Get down on you knees and face the computer.

*(**RICK** gets down on his knees. **RICK'S CONSCIENCE** is still staring at the spilled cereal, so **RICK** pulls him down onto his knees with them.)*

Just hear me out. We're going to pray to the Internet God for help. You spend more time online than you do not, so maybe The Internet God will be able to distract her or, I don't know, stop her from fucking killing us.

RICK. You expect me to believe that there's an Internet God? That sounds like some fully made up shit.

RICK'S LIZARD BRAIN. You have anthropomorphized versions of your lizard brain and your conscience wandering around your fucking apartment and this is where you're going to draw the line on believability?

RICK. Fine.

RICK'S CONSCIENCE. You guys, I'm really not okay.

RICK'S LIZARD BRAIN. Shut up and pray.

RICK. Okay, okay!

> *(All three of them put their hands together and bow their heads, praying to the computer. There's a loud burst of digital sounds as lights rise on the **INTERNET GOD**.)*

> *(The **INTERNET GOD** is represented by two **WOMEN**, both dressed vaguely like Vargas girls surrounded by and somewhat tangled in wires. **INTERNET GOD (2)** is seated on a chair with a hot dog with the works in her hand. **INTERNET GOD (1)** is right next to her on a slightly taller stool with a banana in her hand. They eat the hot dog and banana seductively. It might as well be pornography. It would be great if they were somehow elevated.)*

What in the hell?

> *(The **INTERNET GOD** notices **RICK** and **INTERNET GOD (1)** picks up a nearby megaphone and stands up. **INTERNET GOD (2)** keeps eating and stays seated, but she's paying attention.)*

IG1. "The Internet God has heard your call and appeared. You're welcome."

> *(She curtsies, hands the megaphone to **INTERNET GOD (2)**, and continues to seductively eat her banana.)*

IG2. Very formal, very regal.

IG1. Thanks.

RICK. The Internet God is two slutty chicks eating phallic things?

IG1. Well, okay. Isn't that a wonderful greeting? Tell him I only appear to people as an amalgam of images from their own browser histories and with his explicit tastes and rampant porn addiction this was the closest thing I could get to a classy form.

> (**INTERNET GOD (2)** *nods in agreement then turns the megaphone towards the* **GUYS** *in the apartment.*)

IG2. "Fuck yourself and die."

RICK. Wait, what?

IG1. Tell him I'm very busy and if he needs something he should just get on with it and stop wasting everyone's time.

> (**INTERNET GOD (2)** *nods in agreement then turns the megaphone towards the* **GUYS** *in the apartment.*)

IG2. "Fuck yourself and die."

RICK'S CONSCIENCE. You guys, I know I'm kinda out of it but I feel like this isn't going well.

RICK'S LIZARD BRAIN. Because bitches.

RICK. Look, Internet God, I'm in trouble because of you. I thought the Internet is supposed to be, like, some kind of fucking free speech haven? Now this crazy woman is outside my place waiting to stab me to death.

IG1. Oh my God, this banana is so good [it's unbelievable.]

IG2. [Yes, and this hot] dog is the meatiest thing I've ever had in my mouth.

RICK. Hello?! I'm in the fucking mess because of you!

> (*A new and even more adorable kitten image appears.*)

IG1. There's a lot of blame going around. I wonder how long until he realizes this is his own damn fault? Oh, look! Kittens! How fun.

IG2. Adorable kittens. Oh, he's still waiting for an answer.

IG1. Fine. Tell him he has every right to be a monster on the Internet but then there are real world consequences. Oh, and also that the Internet isn't at all about being fair or helpful or even productive. It's just a mirror.

> *(**INTERNET GOD (2)** nods in agreement then turns the megaphone towards the **GUYS** in the apartment.)*

IG2. "Fuck yourself and die."

RICK'S LIZARD BRAIN. Listen you stupid food slut; we need help and you're gonna give it to us!

RICK'S CONSCIENCE. Oh wow.

> *(The **INTERNET GOD** stares at him in shock. **INTERNET GOD (1)** snatches the megaphone and snaps. The lights pulse and everyone takes notice. **ANN MARIE** looks at her phone and smiles.)*

IG1. "Because you think that's how you speak to a God, I just dumped your entire browser history and all of your personal information onto one hundred and twenty-seven of the largest servers in the world. Enjoy global interconnectivity."

> *(**INTERNET GOD (2)** waves dismissively and reminds **INTERNET GOD (1)** ...)*

IG2. FYAD, FYAD.

IG1. Right, yes. "Also... Fuck yourself and die."

> *(There is another burst of digital noise as the lights go out on the **INTERNET GOD**.*

(**RICK** is in shock. **RICK'S CONSCIENCE** *loses consciousness and collapses onto the floor.* **RICK***'s phone vibrates. He answers.)*

ANN MARIE. Hey, Ann Marie again. Still here, still waiting to kill you, in case you were wondering. So anyway this is amazing. Did you know someone just downloaded all of your personal information [and everything...?]

RICK. [Leave me] alone!

(He hangs up. The most adorable kitten image, hands down, appears.)

RICK'S LIZARD BRAIN. Wow. Everyone knows all of your darkest secrets now. This is intense. And I think your conscience actually fucking died. My, like, fight or flight primitive response thing is kicking in so I'm gonna disappear now.

RICK. What?

RICK'S LIZARD BRAIN. Yep. I'm gonna walk in the other room and just kinda fucking cease to be. Well, I'll be inside your head banging around and shit, but this is too real.

RICK. You're leaving me alone?

RICK'S LIZARD BRAIN. I mean...fuck, man. You were always alone.

*(***RICK'S LIZARD BRAIN*** walks out.* **RICK** *cowers.* **ANN MARIE** *hums and dials again.* **RICK***'s phone rings. He doesn't answer. She keeps calling.)*

End of Play

Cough Syrup

COUGH SYRUP was created for The 24 Hour Plays Viral Monologues (Mark Armstrong, Artistic Director). It premiered in Round 13 on June 23, 2020. The cast was as follows:

RICHIE..Frankie J. Alvarez

CHARACTERS

RICHIE

(**RICHIE** *starts the camera on his phone. He's in the car. He has a plastic bag from the drug store. He's also all worked up as he pulls off his mask. Really this is all amped up. He's trying his best to calm down, but it's clearly not working.*)

RICHIE. Oh my god, that was just...?

(*He looks at the camera.*)

Fuck.

(*He shakes his head. And then he lets loose and we're off!*)

Okay, okay. Okay, Jill. I'm just, I'm still processing. And I know you'll get it, so I'm recording this because it was too fucking crazy and I know later you won't believe me. Fuck. Okay, I'm gonna stop saying fuck. It was – I don't know. Give me a minute.

(*He takes two deep breaths. Then starts laughing and we're off again...*)

There was this woman in the drugstore, not wearing a mask by the way. No mask. And she slapped the shit out of me. No, first she just started yelling at me about buying cough syrup. I don't mean she was, like, a little loud, I mean she was yelling. It's not like – Jill, I didn't even do anything. She just saw the cough syrup and started ranting about how this brand is used by people to drug and kidnap people's pets, which is insane. It's insane, right? Then she started screaming "Kidnapper! Kidnapper!" and I mean what the fuck? Then she slapped me. I was in shock. Like what is happening?

Oh! There she is. There she, she's coming out. You know what, Jill? Fuck it, I'm gonna say something.

(He gets out of the car and yells!)

Hey! Hey, there's nothing wrong with buying cough syrup! There is something wrong with hitting people! Maybe I am gonna kidnap your cat. I bet you have cats, you have to have fucking cats, right?! I'm gonna get them drunk on cough syrup and, like, smuggle them away! And wear a mask, you crazy lady!!

(He gets back in.)

Fuck! Fuck, Jill, I might follow this woman home and drug and kidnap her cat. If she has a cat. You didn't see her, but she has a cat. Fuck, no I'm not. I'm not going to, this is just something crazy that happened. It doesn't mean anything, it's not important. God, why the fuck am I so angry?

(Then his eyes narrow and he says quietly under his breath...)

Maybe I should just run her over.

(He stops.)

(He starts laughing but he doesn't look happy.)

(He looks like he doesn't know what's happening.)

(He grips the steering wheel and tries to stop.)

(More laughing. This is not normal.)

(He suddenly looks over, clearly remembering the camera.)

(Then he looks at his hands. They're shaking.)

I think… No, I think I feel like this all the time. I'm angry all the time and it just buzzes in the background when I'm gardening, barbecuing, when we go to the park. Jill, I literally started planning that woman's funeral in my head. And planning the little funerals for her cats.

Do you feel like this now?

Not the "cats" thing. Do you feel this angry?

Was…was that woman this angry?

Is everyone this angry now?

Jesus, I'm having an existential crisis in my car and all I wanted was cough syrup.

(He takes another deep breath. He shakes it off. He's calmer now.)

Jill, I don't know if I'm going to show you this. You might divorce me and I'd be alone. And if I was alone, I might start kidnapping people's pets for company. I already have the cough syrup. No. I am going to drive home. We're going to watch this together and if you make it this far, you'll tell me if you're angry too or if I'm just crazy. What the fuck is happening?

(He takes the cough syrup out of the bag and looks at it. He reaches over and turns off the video. He leans back and exhales loudly.)

End of Play

Dark Suburban Still Life with Small Figure

DARK SUBURBAN STILL LIFE WITH SMALL FIGURE premiered on October 2, 2023, as a part of The 24 Hour Plays Los Angeles (Mark Armstrong, Artistic Director). The production was directed by Lovell Holder. The cast was as follows:

SIREN... Midori Francis
BECKY...Jolene Purdy
JENNIFER... Jessica Rothe
MATTHEW..................................... Patrick Heusinger

CHARACTERS

- **SIREN** – A woman & mythological beast in a black pencil skirt, black formfitting blouse, red heels, a clutch purse, red lips, hair pulled up. You get the idea.
- **BECKY** – A woman, the Siren's best friend. She's a little bit odd and always carries around a really fucked-up doll. Like the doll has seen some shit.
- **JENNIFER** – A determined young suburban wife in jeans and a cardigan. Sleeves pushed back and a scarf holding her hair as if she's been gardening.
- **MATTHEW** – A hapless young suburban husband in khakis and a bloody shirt. With bloody white bandages over his ears. But he's pretty good with it all.

AUTHOR'S NOTES

CAPS in the script indicate shouting.

You'll need: a clutch purse, a severely messed-up doll, stage blood, a large pair of hedge trimming shears, bandages, gauze, and an old railroad spike.

*(**MATTHEW** yelps in pain offstage. Another yelp. What the fuck?)*

*(The **SIREN**, carrying her clutch, walks up to the door and knocks. **BECKY** follows her, cheerful but carrying a really fucked-up doll. The **SIREN** knocks on the door. Nothing.)*

SIREN. Oh my god, are they fucking serious with this whole "making me wait" thing?

BECKY. It's so crazy.

SIREN. It is crazy. And super rude.

BECKY. It's like, don't they know how you are?

SIREN. Right? Okay, but you said that, not me. I'm humble. But yeah, it's totally fucked up.

*(The **SIREN** knocks on the door again. More forcefully or maybe just for a longer duration. **JENNIFER** enters with a pair of large, bloody hedge clippers. She also has blood splatter on her hands and face.)*

MATTHEW. *(From offstage.)* HURRY BACK, HONEY. I'M MAKING PANCAKES.

JENNIFER. BACK IN A SEC.

(She answers the door.)

Sorry! I was out back. You caught me right in the middle of something.

SIREN. Hmm, not a problem. Is your husband home?

JENNIFER. I'm sorry?

SIREN. Oh, I asked if your husband is home.

BECKY. Super polite.

SIREN. Right?

JENNIFER. Yes, my husband is home. We're about to have pancakes.

SIREN. Could I speak with him, please? Just for a quick minute, just for the tiniest little second.

JENNIFER. May I ask what this is regarding?

BECKY. DO YOU HAVE ANY IDEA WHO YOU'RE TALKING TO?! She is a mythic being, she is the closest thing to magic you'll ever experience in your tiny life, she is perfect! Perfect!!

> (**BECKY** *shoves into the house, causing* **JENNIFER** *to back up and wield her hedge clippers defensively. Whoa.* **BECKY** *went from zero to sixty.*)

SIREN. Whoa. You went from zero to sixty. I've got this.

BECKY. No, totally. Sorry. I shouldn't have had that venti white mocha with a triple shot. I'm just wired.

SIREN. Now, I was asking about your husband because husbands are my area of interest.

JENNIFER. Ah, okay. You're one of those mythical sirens, right? Part bird, part woman? The ones that seductively lure men to their deaths?

SIREN. Oh my god, I'm so embarrassed. This is so embarrassing. You do know who I am. I don't like to assume people will recognize me, I'm quite humble.

BECKY. Everyone says she's humble.

SIREN. People used to paint me.

JENNIFER. Okay well, no one is painting this.

SIREN. You'd be surprised.

JENNIFER. Trust me, no one is going to paint this. Anyway, you've been standing out on the front lawn singing an eerie and enthralling song all morning, and kind of glowing in an incandescent way. So it wasn't hard to piece together your identity.

SIREN. Yes, yes, that's right. I'm a siren. Hi. We used to stick mainly to the sea, smashing ships into rocks and drowning men, all that stuff. But people don't travel by boats as much as they used to, you know? And cruise ships are so loud. It's just really annoying. Anyway – and you are?

JENNIFER. Jennifer. And you're – a siren too?

*(The **SIREN** and **BECKY** laugh. Maybe they even sit down. Maybe not.)*

SIREN. Oh no, Jennifer. This is Becky. She's my best friend. She drove me here in her Prius. It's nice. And it always smells like vanilla, which is so nice.

BECKY. I have a little thing that hangs from the rear-view mirror and makes everything smell like vanilla.

JENNIFER. And that's – and that's – what's wrong with that doll?

BECKY. SHE'S BEEN THROUGH A LOT!! IS THAT OKAY WITH YOU?! FUCK, WE'RE NOT HERE TO TALK ABOUT LITTLE JANESSA ANYWAY! I MEAN JESUS FUCKING CHRIST, WHAT IS YOUR DEAL?!

(Pause. Wow.)

JENNIFER. So – that trainwreck of a doll is named Little Vanessa?

*(**BECKY** smiles –)*

BECKY. It's "Janessa" and I will murder you, Jennifer.

SIREN. Becky, chill. I'm working here. Or else, like, go wait in the Prius.

BECKY. No, I'm good. I'm chill.

> (**MATTHEW** *shouts from the kitchen, out of view...*)

MATTHEW. *(From offstage.)* HONEY, WHAT'S GOING ON IN THERE? THE PANCAKES ARE WAITING.

JENNIFER. NOTHING, BABE. ALL GOOD. BE RIGHT THERE.

MATTHEW. *(From offstage.)* WHAT?

JENNIFER. Oh my god, just ignore him. Matthew is super sweet, but he can't handle anything stressful.

MATTHEW. *(From offstage.)* WHAT DID YOU SAY?

JENNIFER. This entire sort of passive aggressive confrontation would make him so anxious. And Little Janessa is going to give me nightmares. I'm covered in blood and Little Janessa is still the thing that's most likely to give me night terrors.

BECKY. You don't know anything about being a mom.

SIREN. Becky, don't go there. And Jennifer – it seems your husband *is* home.

BECKY. It sure sounds like he *is* home.

MATTHEW. *(From offstage.)* JENNIFER?

JENNIFER. I stood here and told you he was home. I was pretty direct about it. Oh, did you know there was a neighborhood watch bulletin all about you? About how you've been standing on lawns and luring men outside then stabbing them. I read the neighborhood watch bulletins to keep up on dangers in the community. Even though they're full of typos.

SIREN. A full bulletin all about me? Am I blushing? I'm blushing.

JENNIFER. Just for clarity, after singing on the front lawns do you always come to the door to share this, I don't know, breathtaking lack of self-awareness?

SIREN. I'm getting the sense you don't like me very much, Jennifer.

JENNIFER. You're reading that correctly.

SIREN. But I'm nice. And humble.

BECKY. The picture of humble.

JENNIFER. You want to murder my husband with an old, girthy railroad spike.

SIREN. Yes, and it's the oddest thing, usually I sing, and the men come right out to me so I can stab them and be on my way. But I've been out there singing and nothing. It's crazy.

BECKY. It's totally crazy.

SIREN. Now is your husband going to come out here so I can put him in a trance with my gorgeous song and then stab him to death or what? This is taking too long and Becky still has to go to the DMV today. I don't want to make her late.

BECKY. Little Janessa is getting one of those REAL ID cards. I mean, I made an appointment online, but when you get there, they still make you wait. It's so annoying.

JENNIFER. Little Janessa is getting a REAL ID?

BECKY. She travels a lot, it's just easier.

JENNIFER. Should you – do something about her hair first?

BECKY. What's wrong with her hair?

JENNIFER. Okay, this is – I just don't understand the doll thing.

*(The **WOMEN** all stop as **MATTHEW** enters. He is wearing khakis and a blood-spattered*

shirt with blood-soaked bandages taped over each ear. Maybe there's blood running down his neck on both sides. Oh shit.)

MATTHEW. HONEY! DID YOU STILL WANT PANCAKES? OH, I DIDN'T KNOW WE HAD COMPANY. WELCOME! ARE YOU NEW TO THE NEIGHBORHOOD? I'M MATTHEW, IT'S NICE TO MEET YOU.

*(**JENNIFER** turns, smiles and shoulders the large hedge clippers.)*

*(The **SIREN** and **BECKY** are genuinely shocked.)*

SIREN. Holy shit. You cut his ears off so he can't fall under my spell?

*(**MATTHEW** starts to pass out but catches himself on a chair.)*

MATTHEW. YOU'LL HAVE TO SPEAK UP. MY WIFE CUT MY EARS OFF BECAUSE A MYTHOLOGICAL SIREN HAS BEEN ENTHRALLING AND KILLING HUSBANDS IN THE NIEGHBORHOOD. IT'S TOTALLY CRAZY. LIKE FIVE DEAD HUSBANDS SO FAR. SHE USES LIKE A GIANT NAIL OR SOMETHING.

SIREN. That's flattering. But it's not a nail.

MATTHEW. WHAT?

(She opens her clutch and pulls out an old railroad spike.)

SIREN. It's an old railroad spike. It has more heft than a knife. It's more substantial, you know?

BECKY. Little Janessa always says that size matters.

SIREN. Size does matter.

MATTHEW. DIDN'T QUITE CATCH THAT. ONE MORE TIME?

SIREN, BECKY & JENNIFER. SIZE MATTERS!

MATTHEW. SORRY. HAVING TROUBLE HEARING YOU. AND FEELING A LITTLE BIT DIZZY. AND WOOZY. WITH LOVE, PROBABLY. ANYWAY, JENNIFER LOVES ME TOO MUCH TO LET ME GET MURDERED. SHE'S THE BEST. SO WE WENT AHEAD AND TOOK CARE OF IT, RIGHT HONEY? HEY, WHAT'S WRONG WITH THAT UGLY DOLL?

BECKY. SHE'S LIVED A FULL LIFE, OKAY? SHE'S A SURVIVOR! YOU CAN GO FUCK YOURSELF AND DIE, THERE IS NOTHING IS WRONG WITH HER!

MATTHEW. ARE THOSE BUGS IN HER HAIR?

JENNIFER. There are fully bugs in her hair, Becky.

BECKY. And you maimed your husband, Jennifer. You are a stone-cold bitch.

JENNIFER. I've literally been covered with blood holding a giant pair of hedge clippers this entire time. I'm the Veruca Salt of this house. I get what I want when I want it.

SIREN. Who the fuck is Veruca Salt?

BECKY. Veruca Salt is a selfish little girl from the book *Charlie and the Chocolate Factory* by Roald Dahl who demands things and whines and then gets pushed down an incinerator shaft by squirrels.

MATTHEW. JENNIFER ALWAYS SAYS SHE'S THE VERUCA SALT OF THIS HOUSE. BUT A HAPPY WIFE MEANS A HAPPY LIFE, RIGHT? HONEY, AFTER WE FINISH THE PANCAKES THEN WE MIGHT NEED TO GO TO THE HOSPITAL. I THINK I LOST A LOT OF BLOOD.

JENNIFER. FOR SURE, BABE. WILL YOU PUT SOME EXTRA SYRUP ON MINE?

MATTHEW. LOVE YOU.

JENNIFER. LOVE YOU, TOO.

MATTHEW. I'LL TOTALLY GET THOSE PANCAKES SOON, BUT I'M JUST GOING TO PASS OUT FOR A MINUTE.

> (**MATTHEW** *smiles and collapses onto the floor.*)

JENNIFER. Ugh, we had to do all this just because of you. Now we have to go to the hospital. You're just the worst kind of homewrecker.

SIREN. Of course I am. It's kind of my thing. But you really take the cake. I mean how fucked up is this?

BECKY. So fucked up.

JENNIFER. You were going to kill him.

SIREN. Right, but there's a limit. I mean, I got blood on my shoes. There's a limit.

BECKY. There's a limit, Jennifer.

JENNIFER. Well sorry to disappoint you, Siren. I think our love is just a little bit too strong for you. Better luck with someone else's husband.

MATTHEW. WAIT. BABE, I'M OKAY NOW. READY FOR THOSE PANCAKES?

JENNIFER. SURE AM, BABE!

> (**MATTHEW** *struggles to get up. Blood sprays from* **MATTHEW**'s *ear! It's a torrent. He falls to the floor again, unconscious.*)

SIREN. Huh. You win this round, young suburban housewife. Let's get out of here, Becky.

BECKY. Okay. Oooh, maybe they'll have some men you can kill at the DMV.

SIREN. Nice. Loving that optimism.

End Play

Everything That Happened Before That Terrible Holiday Sweater Party

EVERYTHING THAT HAPPENED BEFORE THAT TERRIBLE HOLIDAY SWEATER PARTY opened on December 6, 2018, as a part of the Winter Shorts Festival at Carnival Studio Theatre, Adrienne Arsht Center for the Performing Arts. It was commissioned by City Theatre (Margaret Ledford, Artistic Director) in Miami, FL. The production was directed by Margaret Ledford. The cast was as follows:

SALLY . . . . Daryl Patrice
MATTHEW . . . . Alex Alvarez
CAROLERS . . . . Dave Cory, Jovon Jacobs,
            Erin Wilbanks & Auberth Bercy

CHARACTERS

- **SALLY** – a wife, not the biggest fan of the holidays, usually preoccupied by current events
- **MATTHEW** – a husband, the kind of guy who brings a fruitcake to a holiday party then gets drunk
- **CAROLERS** – a company of good-natured people going door to door, singing festive songs, and spreading joy & good cheer for the holidays

AUTHOR'S NOTES

This all moves very quickly. It's fast and fun. It's not thoughtful.

SALLY's "holiday sweater" should vaguely resemble a reindeer but honestly it should be a tacky mess. Bonus points if it lights up.

The **CAROLERS** always speak in unison.

(**SALLY** *is in the living room of her apartment. Waiting. She's standing with a remote in her hand, watching the television.* Notably, she's wearing a really terrible holiday sweater. It's overtly awful. Is that supposed to look like a reindeer on it? Honestly, it's hard to tell. And the whole thing might be the wrong size.)*

(The doorbell rings. She flips off the television.)

MATTHEW. *(From offstage.)* Was that the doorbell? Who is it?

SALLY. I don't know yet. Just finish getting ready.

*(She opens the door. A group of **CAROLERS** are there. She barely has the door open when they shout at her with glee! She is startled.)*

CAROLERS. Happy Holidays!!

SALLY. Oh!

CAROLERS. Sorry. Didn't mean to startle you.

SALLY. You're fine. I'm sorry.

CAROLERS. We used to say "Merry Christmas."

SALLY. Okay...?

CAROLERS. But now we don't. Maybe that's why you look horrified?

---

* A license to produce *Everything That Happened Before That Terrible Holiday Sweater Party* does not include a performance license for any third-party or copyrighted recordings or images. Licensees must acquire rights for any copyrighted recordings or images or create their own.

SALLY. Oh no! No, I'm just all wired from watching the evening news. It makes me so anxious, you know? And we just, um, we don't usually have carolers inside the apartment building. Like this. How did you get in?

CAROLERS. We know the door guy.

SALLY. Ah. Well, we're just getting ready to head out to a holiday party actually. So unfortunately, we'll have to miss out this year.

CAROLERS. Aww, so not even time for one song?

SALLY. Sorry.

> *(They start singing "God Rest Ye Merry Gentlemen.")*

Oh no, I meant that I don't...

> *(They keep singing.)*

Have a wonderful evening. And a lovely holiday.

> *(Still singing.)*

I'm closing the door now.

> *(She closes the door. They stop.)*

MATTHEW. *(From offstage.)* Was it Santa?

SALLY. Stop asking me things and finish getting ready. We're late! We're always late and everyone laughs when you tell them how it takes me forever to get ready even though it's really you and isn't that "ha ha" funny while I stand here waiting again?

> *(**MATTHEW** is dressed nice and looking good as he rushes in.)*

MATTHEW. Sorry, what did you say?

SALLY. I said it was a group of carolers at the door, but I sent them away.

MATTHEW. Bah humbug.

SALLY. Yep, that's me. Are you ready to go?

MATTHEW. I'm sorry. I'm the worst, okay? If I hadn't waited to stop by the store to get our gift then I wouldn't have been behind and we wouldn't be late.

SALLY. A fruitcake is not a gift. It's barely even food.

MATTHEW. Um, fruitcakes are universally loved. Who doesn't love a fruitcake?

SALLY. I don't.

MATTHEW. I know. But you tolerate them. For me. And I adore you for it.

SALLY. Just don't tell everyone it's my fault we're late. Because it's not.

MATTHEW. If they really knew us, they'd know it's my fault.

SALLY. Nobody really knows anyone.

MATTHEW. Whoa.

SALLY. I don't know, was that too existential?

MATTHEW. What is this dark mood? Ah, you were watching the evening news again weren't you?

SALLY. I like to stay informed about the end of all good things. And the weather.

MATTHEW. This is my fault for running behind.

SALLY. It's fine. We're only a little bit late.

MATTHEW. Is this a thing where I'm late and you say, "It's fine" and then punish me for the rest of the night?

SALLY. I don't know yet. Enjoy the suspense.

> (**MATTHEW** *kisses* **SALLY**. *It's sweet. She smiles and grabs her purse. He finally notices the sweater.*)

MATTHEW. Oh fuck.

SALLY. What did you forget?

MATTHEW. No, it's just I need to change.

SALLY. Why? We're already late and you look fine. You look nice.

MATTHEW. Come on, Sally. You didn't tell me it was one of those terrible holiday sweater parties. I'm gonna look stupid if I don't go change.

SALLY. It isn't one of those terrible holiday sweater parties.

(Pause. And it's a loaded pause.)

MATTHEW. I love you.

SALLY. You can go to hell.

MATTHEW. Sally.

SALLY. I didn't even want to go to this party in the first place, you know I don't like holiday parties. I mean the world is basically on fire, people are doing insane things, and we're going to go toast some mythical baby and you think my sweater is a gag sweater or intentionally ugly or whatever.

MATTHEW. Mythical baby?

SALLY. What's wrong with my sweater?

MATTHEW. Nothing. Is…is that supposed to be a reindeer?

SALLY. I swear to god.

MATTHEW. Nothing's wrong with it.

SALLY. I know nothing's wrong with it.

MATTHEW. It's a really "fun" sweater.

SALLY. And I can "hear" the air quotes around the word "fun."

MATTHEW. I'm late and I'm an asshole, okay?

SALLY. And?

MATTHEW. And you don't have to toast to a mythical baby.

SALLY. And?

MATTHEW. Oh, and I really like your very appropriate and demure holiday sweater.

SALLY. Fine.

(The doorbell rings. **SALLY** *answers it. The* **CAROLERS** *scare her again!)*

CAROLERS. Happy Holidays!!

SALLY. Oh my god!

MATTHEW. Happy holidays, folks.

CAROLERS. We thought you were leaving?

SALLY. We are.

CAROLERS. We waited to see if you were telling the truth. Tis the season for misleading people and being a real downer.

MATTHEW. Whoa. Don't talk like that to my wife. You're being very impolite.

(The **CAROLERS** *put up their fists to fight.)*

CAROLERS. You wanna go, pal?

SALLY. Matthew, there's too many of them.

CAROLERS. You know what they say: when mistletoe doesn't work, you can always just use a baseball bat.

SALLY. Nobody says that!

MATTHEW. Does, okay, does one of you have a bat?

SALLY. What happened to spreading cheer? This is exactly the problem with modern society! No one knows how to have a civil discourse anymore! No one is civil!!

CAROLERS. You're shouting.

SALLY. I know I'm shouting!!

MATTHEW. Listen, let's deescalate this situation. It's not my wife's fault that she's, oh, we're not going to fight, you can put down your fists. Thank you. Now, it's not her fault that the holidays bring out her anxiety and misanthropy.

SALLY. They certainly do not.

MATTHEW. She doesn't know.

SALLY. Don't tell them that.

CAROLERS. We're sorry. We didn't realize.

MATTHEW. Hey, don't worry. We all have our holiday baggage, right?

CAROLERS. Well, the least we could do is sing for you.

SALLY. Absolutely not.

CAROLERS. Fine. But it's cold out. Could we at least have something warm to drink?

SALLY. You're in the hallway of an apartment building!

(She slams the door on them.)

MATTHEW. Honey. Let's just take some deep breaths and remember what this season of joy and love is all about. It's about joy and love.

SALLY. Ugh, I just hate that so much, that exact thing with the carolers. Everyone pretends to be nice when no one is really nice anymore.

MATTHEW. Okay. Okay, so maybe think of it like this: Even if they're just pretending, and I don't think everyone is, but even if the holidays are all just an act, isn't that a nice respite from all of the anger and craziness in the world today? Come on, Christmas stockings hung with care are at least a little bit better than the collapse of western civilization, right?

(Pause.)

SALLY. Maybe...and I'm saying maybe...maybe I see your point. A tiny bit.

MATTHEW. It's a holiday miracle.

SALLY. Can we just go before they come back?

MATTHEW. Absolutely. Let me just grab the fruitcake I bought.

SALLY. Oh, I threw it in the trash.

MATTHEW. You did not.

SALLY. You look like I just shot someone.

MATTHEW. Listen, I'm the jerk tonight and I get that, but you had to throw my fruitcake in the trash?

SALLY. I threw the store-bought fruitcake in the trash. Yes. I had to do it, okay? And I know how much you love fruitcake, but we'll get something else on the way to the party.

MATTHEW. Sally, that fruitcake was for the party! I bring fruitcakes, it's my thing.

SALLY. Trust me, I know.

MATTHEW. That was a lot of judgment in a very short sentence.

SALLY. Look, they said on the news that someone at the grocery store was caught on the security camera, um, I don't want to say it.

*(**SALLY** awkwardly mimes her idea of a man masturbating. It's odd.)*

MATTHEW. I do not understand the gestures you are making right now.

SALLY. They caught someone, eh hm, "masturbating" on the fruitcakes.

MATTHEW. Come on.

SALLY. Yes. Apparently he was rubbing himself on all of them. All of them. And then he, you know…finished on them.

MATTHEW. Oh wow. Hold on, they showed that on the local news?

SALLY. Of course not, but they described it.

MATTHEW. Oh. That's less shocking.

SALLY. No, it's not. And he was wearing a Santa mask. The world is a sick place. So I put on a pair of oven mitts and threw the fruitcake away. To be safe.

MATTHEW. Well, that's wasteful. We can still take that perfectly good fruitcake to the party. I'll go get it out of the trash.

SALLY. Matthew! No we cannot.

MATTHEW. Oh no, no, I think that one's fine. I can tell.

SALLY. Because you're some fruitcake expert, right?

MATTHEW. No. Because I picked that one out special before I rubbed my dick on all the other ones on the shelf in that store.

SALLY. What?

MATTHEW. I picked that one out special before I rubbed my dick on all the other ones on the shelf in that store.

SALLY. Matthew.

MATTHEW. Oh no, don't look upset, it's really not a big deal. I'm the same man you married. I just feel like I should confess to you in case they have footage of me on the security tapes putting on the Santa mask. I just, I got so excited that I didn't even think to look for cameras. Oh, and I didn't mean to "finish" on them, I just really love fruitcake.

SALLY. You had sex with a bunch of fruitcakes?!

MATTHEW. Honey, I don't think you really understand how much I love fruitcake. Maybe you're right. Maybe nobody really knows anyone.

(He looks out wistfully. Profound. She is fully in shock.)

SALLY. But I know you. I've...I've known you since I was sixteen.

MATTHEW. Sure, but I started doing the fruitcake thing when I was twelve. It started off as a dare from a classmate. That's not true, I just wanted do it.

SALLY. Every year?

MATTHEW. The holidays are such a magical time.

SALLY. Oh god, I hate this time of year so much. I think I might be sick.

MATTHEW. You'll be okay once we get you a slice of fruitcake and a yummy glass of eggnog. Are you sure I don't have time to put on a "fun" sweater?

End of Play

Fluff

FLUFF premiered on May 2, 2024, as a part of *Distractions at the Crash Site, an Evening of Steve Yockey Short Plays* at Theatre of Note in Los Angeles, CA. The production was directed by Ryan Bergmann. The cast was as follows:

GABE . . . . Joel Scher
BUNNY . . . . Ron Morehouse
BLUEBIRD . . . . Trevor Olsen
CHORUS . . . . Grace Eboigbe, Sierra Marcks & Gabby Sanalitro

CHARACTERS

GABE – a man, all self-conscious laughter and nervous energy, deeply frustrated while trying hard to unpack a series of terrible events, one of them being his relationship

BUNNY – a person in a fitted suit wearing a giant bunny head with "X"s for eyes and maybe even a halo, because the bunny is dead

BLUEBIRD – a person in a fitted suit wearing a giant bluebird head with "X"s for eyes and maybe even a halo, because the bluebird is dead

CHORUS – a group, a modern take on a Greek chorus

AUTHOR'S NOTES

[ ] in the script indicate overlapping dialogue.

The play is not sentimental (until the end) and moves at pace.

The red glitter confetti in the final moment is an ideal and may be achieved in other ways. Whatever the solution, it should be messy.

The **CHORUS** always speaks in unison.

(**GABE** *is standing onstage. He doesn't exactly look thrilled to be there. A* **CHORUS** *of people is also present onstage. They're waiting for* **GABE** *to start.*)

(**GABE** *begins to say something to the* **CHORUS**. *He stops. He laughs at himself like he can't believe this. He musters determination, then...*)

GABE. Fuck. Okay, just... Fuck it, do you believe in ghosts?

CHORUS. No.

GABE. Good. Good, me either. That's good. It's just... Okay, the ghost of a bunny rabbit is currently haunting me. A bunny rabbit my boyfriend killed.

CHORUS. This is Gabe. His boyfriend killed a bunny rabbit.

GABE. Accidentally killed.

CHORUS. This is Gabe. He does not believe in ghosts.

GABE. Right, but my position on that is sort of "evolving." And to be clear, I don't think the bunny ghost is going to hurt me. Physically. But it's not happy. I mean obviously it's not happy about being dead.

CHORUS. This is Gabe. He read on the Internet that some people think ghosts are spirits who stick around when they have unfinished business.

GABE. Sure. Okay. I did read that. It's unsettling.

CHORUS. Not to us because we don't believe in ghosts.

GABE. It's frustrating. I don't exactly know all the details. I walked into my bedroom last week and there was a smell. Like, a bad smell. Which, I mean, I use those refillable plug-in things to keep the entire house smelling like "beach mist," which only sort of smells like the beach. Anyway, this was some other very bad smell. So I looked everywhere and then, under the bed, I found the box.

CHORUS. Ominous.

GABE. It was, yeah.

CHORUS. But we're a tragic chorus so we wouldn't be here if things were nice.

GABE. Sure, sure. So I look inside the box and see a dead bunny. With some carrots and a little bowl of water. And it did not smell like the beach.

CHORUS. No.

GABE. And when my boyfriend Benjamin came home from rock climbing, I confronted him. He's a great guy, there are issues and we maybe shouldn't be together, but he's great.

CHORUS. This is Gabe. He's learning relationships are hard.

GABE. Anyway, I confront him about the secret box. He explains that he hit this rabbit with his car and he felt terrible about it, so he thought maybe he could nurse it back to health. Ask me if he's a veterinarian?

CHORUS. Is he a veterinarian?

GABE. He is a salesman at a paper company. Now ask me if he has a severe rescue complex and an infuriating need to step into difficult situations?

CHORUS. Does he have a [severe...]

GABE. [Yes, he] does. Thank you for asking. And the sad part is that the bunny had clearly died at this point, probably upon impact. But Benjamin thought maybe it was in a coma, like a little, fluffy coma, and just needed time to recover. And he secretly put it under the bed, and I'm quoting him now: "So that bright light wouldn't scare it when it woke up."

CHORUS. "When?"

GABE. He's optimistic that way. It just, it really makes me tired.

CHORUS. Well, those are all thoughtful things at least.

GABE. You think so? Because I think the bunny did not think it was thoughtful. and that's why it's haunting our house. I sort of see it around corners or at the top of the stairs. Lurking. Plotting something. And it's…bigger.

CHORUS. It's probably just a psychic manifestation of your feelings of guilt.

GABE. But I don't have anything to feel guilty about!

CHORUS. Whoa.

GABE. Or I shouldn't have to feel guilty or sad or any of the other things a ghost wants you to feel. I buried that bunny in the backyard under the maple tree and said a nice little prayer. And I'm not even religious.

>   (**BUNNY** *enters behind* **GABE**. **BUNNY** *is in a fitted suit and has a giant rabbit head with "X"s for eyes and maybe even a halo. The* **CHORUS** *can see* **BUNNY** *from their position, but* **GABE** *cannot.* **BUNNY** *quietly stares at* **GABE**. *Intense.*)

CHORUS. So Gabe, we don't want to [alarm you…]

GABE. [No, I'm very] aware you're probably thinking, "Oh, this is an isolated incident and Gabe's blowing this way out of proportion, even if the ghost part is true. Animals die so what's the big deal?"

CHORUS. We sort of were, but also maybe you should [look behind…]

GABE. [Because honestly] what can a ghost bunny rabbit really do to me other than hop around adorably? And also maybe make me question all of my big life choices while it slowly drives me to the brink of madness.

CHORUS. This is Gabe. Spiraling faster than we initially thought.

*(**BUNNY** is still fixated on **GABE**.)*

GABE. I'm not spiraling. Or fine, whatever, but let me be clear that this is not an isolated incident. In my relationship. In the pet cemetery that is my relationship. Ugh, can I just tell you about the terrible thing that happened last month? Look, I'm going to tell you about the terrible thing that happened last month.

Benjamin comes running inside and says I have to come out to the, like, carport thing. He practically drags me out there. He seriously almost pulled my arm out of the socket and I was scared to death.

But when I get outside, there's a bluebird. This bluebird with, I don't want to call it a broken wing; that would be a huge understatement. The bird is really hurt. Benjamin found it in the driveway, injured, and tried to help it. Like he's remotely capable of providing medical care to a bluebird. This is the whole rescue complex, who does this?

And the poor bluebird was clearly terrified. So once Benjamin got it into the garage it just kept flying into the wall over and over like some kind of demented house fly until it fell in the corner.

So we're standing there looking at the bluebird and I'm waiting. Until finally he says, "We have to put it out of its misery."

CHORUS. Uh-oh.

GABE. That's right "Uh-oh." Immediately, I think, "Fuck." Because he doesn't mean "we" have to put it out of its misery, he wants me to do it. I'm supposed to, I don't know, "euthanize" the bluebird in the carport.

So I ask him, "Okay, Benjamin. What should we use to kill the bird?"

And he says: "Gabe. We're not killing it; we're giving it peace!"

And I say: "I'm gonna hit it with a shovel, okay?"

And I swear to you, he had this expression. I say this thing about the shovel to him and his eyes go wide like he's never heard of anything so horrible as smashing a bluebird with a shovel.

> (**BLUEBIRD** *enters behind* **GABE**. **BLUEBIRD** *is in a fitted suit and has a giant bird head with "X"s for eyes and maybe even a little halo, a bucket, and a shovel. Again the* **CHORUS** *can see* **BLUEBIRD**, *but* **GABE** *cannot.* **BLUEBIRD** *stands next to* **BUNNY**. *They both stare at* **GABE**.)

And honestly, in that moment, I wanted to punch him right in the face. And maybe he teared up but I couldn't or I didn't, I mean someone has deal with the situation. So I used my foot to sort of kick the bird out of the corner, out into the open, and I smashed it with the shovel.

It only took one swing, but I hit it a bunch of times just to make sure it wasn't hurting. It was sad. It was not a fun task. And then I buried it. We buried the bunny next to it. And there...there are others.

> (**BLUEBIRD** *hands the shovel and bucket to* **BUNNY**. *It points at* **GABE**, *draws a finger across the throat, and then exits.*)

CHORUS. This is Gabe. Honestly, he just told a fucked-up story.

GABE. I just don't know how much more I can take. I don't want to leave him for being nice, but all of his good deeds are taking me to a really dark place. He's taking me to a dark place with fucking bunny ghosts.

CHORUS. This is Gabe. He roped us into some dark shit and now we're kind of on the hook in that socially uncomfortable way where we can't leave, but the conversation unexpectedly escalated. And also ghosts.

GABE. In our backyard, buried under the maple tree, there's a mouse. A possum. A snake. A turtle. Oh, and hand to God, a really expensive parrot named Mr. Prettyfeathers. Which I can't even get into, I can't get into the parrot. I taught him how to say, "I love you, Gabe."

> (**GABE** *clearly loved Mr. Prettyfeathers.*)

And now this ghost is haunting me. I guess for enabling my well-intentioned but clearly dangerous boyfriend. He has a big heart and now I can't even look at him without thinking about all of those poor animals. He cries every time but then moves on. I don't cry, I just feel terrible.

CHORUS. It sounds like he gets to be nice.

And then you have to be kind.

GABE. Is that…holy shit, is that what it is?

CHORUS. So the timing of what we're about to say is bad because you're on the cusp of realizing that you're in the wrong relationship [and we…]

GABE. [Wait, what] now?

CHORUS. But look behind you.

> (**GABE** *is confused. He looks behind him. He sees* **BUNNY**.)

GABE. Oh my god!

*(He covers his eyes with his hands. The **BUNNY** steps closer to him.)*

Is it gone?

CHORUS. This is Gabe. He knows the bunny rabbit's still there.

GABE. Damn it. What the fuck does it want? What does it even want?

*(He keeps his eyes covered. **BUNNY** steps closer and suddenly splashes **GABE** with red glitter confetti from the bucket.)*

*(The **CHORUS** is stunned. **GABE** is stunned. What the fuck?)*

*(Suddenly **BLUEBIRD** runs across the stage at full speed with a bucket and splashes **GABE** again with even more red glitter confetti before rushing off again. It's basically a "drive by" confetti assault.)*

*(**GABE** starts to cry.)*

*(**BUNNY** hesitates. This was unexpected. Then...**BUNNY** hugs **GABE**.)*

End of Play

Go Get 'em, Tiger!

GO GET 'EM, TIGER! opened on June 2, 2022, as a part of the 25th Summer Shorts Festival at Carnival Studio Theatre, Adrienne Arsht Center for the Performing Arts. It was commissioned by City Theatre (Margaret Ledford, Artistic Director) in Miami, FL. The production was directed by Michael Yawney. The cast was as follows:

JOHN . . . . Alex Alvarez
LINDA . . . . Lindsey Corey
ZOOKEEPER . . . . Daniel Llaca
TIGER . . . . Jovon Jacobs

CHARACTERS

JOHN – a husband
LINDA – a wife
ZOOKEEPER – a zoo employee
TIGER – a tiger

AUTHOR'S NOTES

[ ] in the script indicate overlapping dialogue.

This all moves very quickly. It's energetic and fun. And then it drops in and gets very real. And then the tiger shows up and gets surreal, so just enjoy the ride.

The character of **TIGER** is a man in a tiger suit. Please do not use a real tiger, even if you have access to one. It's very dangerous and we won't understand any of his lines anyway.

*(**JOHN** is seated in one of the many available chairs in some kind of holding room. He is has a bag of ice to his head and his shirt is torn. He looks like he knows he's in trouble. Linda's oversized purse is in a chair next to him.)*

*(**LINDA** is up and pacing. She has an ICEE in her hand that she sips from aggressively.* After a moment...)*

JOHN. You're going to get "brain freeze" if you drink that ICEE too fast.

LINDA. Well, it's melting, all right? And I don't want to just drink syrup and water. I know that's all it is anyway, but that's not the point. I don't want to know what is really in this thing, okay? I want to be fooled by this drink. I want this drink to lie to me.

JOHN. I'm just expressing my concern [that you'll...]

LINDA. [You're concerned] about me?!

*(Pause. **LINDA** collects herself. She didn't mean to yell.)*

I did not mean to yell.

JOHN. It's fine. We can just sit quietly until they come back.

*(But **LINDA** can't sit. And she can't be quiet.)*

---

* A license to produce *Go Get 'em, Tiger!* does not include a license to publicly display any branded logos or trademarked images. Licensees must acquire rights for any logos and/or images or create their own.

LINDA. No. I can't sit. And I can't be quiet. Okay, John. Okay. Okay, I've been trying. I've been pacing and trying really hard but I do not understand.

JOHN. Here we go.

LINDA. That's right "here we go" because I've been running it over and over in my head. And I just don't understand. Can you please explain it to me again before we have to explain it to the police? Because assuming you're not too injured, the police will definitely be talking to us. Honestly, I never in a million years thought I [would be…]

JOHN. [Look, you] dropped your purse in so I climbed over the barrier and went down to get it. I don't see what's so complicated.

LINDA. It was the tiger enclosure?

JOHN. Yes, but I'm also nimble. I'm a very nimble guy, so I figured I could get it.

LINDA. You are not nimble.

*(Suddenly **JOHN** stands up like he's going into battle.)*

JOHN. Look, don't tell me what I am and am not. Maybe I've just never demonstrated my nimbleness to you, did you ever think about that? Maybe there are things you don't know about me. Maybe there's an ocean of things you don't know about me.

LINDA. John.

JOHN. What?

LINDA. It was the tiger enclosure!!!

(He recoils and sits again. She brings the volume back down, but is still clearly working through her feelings. She's pacing again.)

The zoo put up large signs to remind people that they shouldn't climb into the animal enclosures. In case a person, like you for instance, has some kind of psychotic episode and common sense just leaves them.

JOHN. If they were serious about keeping people out of there then they would have made it more difficult to get in. That seems pretty [obvious to me.]

   (**LINDA** *stops pacing. Really?*)

LINDA. [You thought] my stupid purse was [so important?]

JOHN. [It's not even] [about the purse.]

LINDA. [John, was the] purse so important?

JOHN. We were having a great day. It was almost the perfect romantic day, wasn't it? Perfect. And then you dropped your purse in the tiger enclosure and you were upset and I didn't want anything to screw it up.

LINDA. So you did it for me?

JOHN. Obviously. Yes.

LINDA. Well, congratulations. Your plan to not screw up our day went so well. Is this how you imagined it? Because this holding room is pretty screwed up. The Zoo security team armed with Tasers and the looming potential legal action is screwed up. Your potential death was really [screwed up.]

JOHN. [I was trying] to be, I don't know, chivalrous. And if you'd stop being mad for two minutes you'd see that I was just trying to impress you.

LINDA. Impress me? Jesus, John, we've been married for seven years. You don't have to impress me anymore.

JOHN. Are you sure I don't need to [impress you?]

LINDA. [What would I] do if you were mauled [by some tiger?!]

JOHN. [It seems like maybe] I do [need to impress you.]

LINDA. [You could have been] killed, John. You could [have been...]

JOHN. [Look, Linda, I] know you're having an affair.

> *(Pause. She stops pacing.)*
>
> *(She starts to speak but stops.)*
>
> *(She sits down in the nearest chair, but not next to him.)*
>
> *(She looks at him.)*
>
> *(He looks at her, waiting.)*
>
> *(She looks like she might cry as it sinks in.)*
>
> *(But she stops herself and pulls it together.)*

LINDA. That's... An affair? That's the stupidest thing to say, John. I mean, it's just a stupid thing to say. Why would I have an affair? There's no reason for me to have an affair? I wouldn't. I'm happy, I'm perfectly happy.

JOHN. Linda, stop.

LINDA. I'm just incredibly happy and content with my, with our, I mean with this, with what we have together.

JOHN. Sure. Okay. That was very convincing, I want to credit you with that. But also I kind of feel like you're actually not incredibly happy.

LINDA. Well, I don't really think that's...

> *(She stands up then sits back down. She honestly looks like she doesn't know what to do.)*

Well no one's incredibly happy all the time. I'm sure you've noticed that the world's not a happy place, John.

Especially when your husband risks his life over a purse. And beyond this incident, there are, just, every day there are little, I don't know, little chips in my, in a person's happiness. And I remind myself no one ever promised me happiness in every single moment, how could they? I mean, no one can just be relentlessly happy day in and day out. Unless you get one of those ice pick lobotomies to just wander around high on hard drugs. So I'm happy enough and just take that at face value and stop accusing me of things.

JOHN. All of that makes sense.

LINDA. Good.

JOHN. I get it.

LINDA. What a relief.

JOHN. But also his name is Matt, he's younger and in better shape than me, he works at the hardware store in the lighting department, he drives a relatively new model Toyota 4Runner, and he says he loves you a lot in text messages. He doesn't use emojis, he actually takes the time to write out "I love you." So he really means it.

(Pause.)

LINDA. I wouldn't, oh my god, I wouldn't put too much stock in the emoji part. He's just not good with phones.

JOHN. Well, that's a relief.

LINDA. How long have you known?

JOHN. Three months.

(This crushes her. That long?)

LINDA. I decided I was only going to tell you if it became something serious. If it wasn't something serious then it could just be a bad thing I did and not something you should have to carry around. Does that make sense?

JOHN. Would he climb into a tiger enclosure for you?

LINDA. I hope not.

JOHN. Do you love him?

> *(Pause. It honestly looks like **LINDA** doesn't know. Just then the door opens and a **ZOOKEEPER** comes in.)*

LINDA. Oh, thank god.

> *(**LINDA** stands and turns away, quickly pulling herself together.)*

ZOOKEEPER. Oh. I didn't mean to interrupt. I don't really care because you broke our rules and put yourself in danger, but socially I'm supposed to apologize for interrupting, right?

JOHN. It's fine.

ZOOKEEPER. Good. I don't really care, but that's good.

LINDA. How long to we have to wait in here?

ZOOKEEPER. We've never had anyone do anything this reckless, so we're still figuring it out. It's throwing a wrench in the whole day and also it's certifiable. Like I said, I really don't care, but are you on some kind of medication?

JOHN. Listen, Zookeeper, have you ever been betrayed by someone you love?

LINDA. I told him it was a crazy thing to do.

ZOOKEEPER. It was remarkably crazy thing to do.

LINDA. And he knows it was crazy, he knows it.

JOHN. Okay, let's just calm down.

ZOOKEEPER. While we finish up the paperwork, thanks again for that, there's actually someone here who wants to speak with you.

JOHN. I don't...what? We were actually in the middle of a pretty difficult conversation and [if we could...]

LINDA. [It's fine; it's totally] fine, our chat can wait. It can definitely wait.

JOHN. Linda, I'd like an answer [to my question.]

LINDA. [You don't want to] be rude, John. Goodness. Not after you've already put these people out today.

JOHN. Oh, Linda. This is juts...it's just disappointing.

ZOOKEEPER. Great. I'm glad it's okay. I mean, I was going to bring him in anyway, just so we're clear. Because I really don't care what you want or think.

> (**JOHN** and **LINDA** exchange a confused look.)

You can come in now.

> (A **TIGER** enters the holding room. **JOHN** and **LINDA** immediately scream and rush to the far side of the room. **LINDA** throws her ICEE at the **TIGER**, but misses very badly.)

JOHN. [What is this?! You can't let a tiger in here?!]

LINDA. [Oh my, oh my god!! Why would you do that?!]

> (**JOHN** puts himself in front of **LINDA**, protectively.)

ZOOKEEPER. See? That's the healthy fear that's supposed to keep you from climbing into the enclosures. I'll give you a minute.

TIGER. Thanks.

> (The **ZOOKEEPER** leaves. The **TIGER** stands there. **JOHN** and **LINDA** are breathing hard and terrified. What's going to happen?)

Do you mind if I sit? Cat got your tongue? That's just some light humor.

*(**LINDA** lets out one sharp, punctuated scream. The **TIGER** takes a seat.)*

TIGER. Okay, have it your way. Listen, after the tranquilizers wore off, I asked if I could speak with you for a minute. Usually I'm not allowed because of the whole large predatory cat thing, but they made an exception. And by the way, I'm not sure why I'm the one that got shot with a tranquilizer gun. You were the crazy stranger breaking into my house.

JOHN. I'm sorry. I got…they got me with a Taser gun. It hurt, if that helps any.

LINDA. John, stop talking to the tiger.

JOHN. I'm not going to be rude. He's not doing anything. He's way over there.

LINDA. That's his game. He's sneaky.

TIGER. He's also right here and can clearly hear you. Wow. Anyway, I'm twenty-five years old. That's no big deal to you, but most tigers live for around sixteen years. So basically I'm over one hundred and I'm really wise, okay?

JOHN. That's impressive.

TIGER. I appreciate that you're humoring me, but it is actually very impressive. And I've had a long time to watch people coming and going from the zoo. I'm very curious. It's basically all I do now besides eat, sleep, and play with this big rubber ball with a bell in it that just drives me fucking nuts.

(He mimes playing with the rubber ball and gets excited.)

Sorry, I get distracted. But I was watching through the two-way mirror over there and I have a question.

*(**LINDA** is scandalized. **JOHN** is clearly embarrassed.)*

LINDA. Why does a zoo have a two-way mirror?! You were watching us?! Why were you, are other people, is there some kind of audience back there? I told you, John. I told you that tiger had some kind of game.

JOHN. Oh my god, this is so humiliating.

TIGER. Linda, please calm down. John, don't be embarrassed. I'm just curious by nature, I only wanted to ask Linda a question.

LINDA. Me? Why me? Is something bad going to happen? Oh god, is this a trap?

TIGER. No, now, I'm just curious. Like I said, twenty-five human years is a long time to do the same thing every day. And sometimes I feel unfulfilled, and sometimes I'm unhappy, and sometimes I want a change, because that's how we're all built. So the question I want to ask you, Linda, and sorry it's so personal. But after watching you together, did you fall out of love with John or do you just want a change?

LINDA. I'm...huh. You can't just... I'm not answering your silly tiger question.

(**JOHN** *walks over and sits down next to the* **TIGER**. *They both look at* **LINDA**. **JOHN** *crosses his arms.* **LINDA** *looks very uncomfortable.*)

TIGER. Linda, just be honest. In my experience, again twenty-five years old here, honesty is the best policy. And I'm [so curious.]

LINDA. [Yeah, I get] it, you're curious. You don't have to keep repeating it.

JOHN. We're both curious.

LINDA. Fine. Fine. That's fine. Well, I guess I thought I was in a rut and just wanted something new. And Matt from the hardware store was something new. And exciting. And he installed our new outdoor lighting, so that was a plus. But I don't love Matt. And a marriage is supposed to be forever. I know that. And I mean, I clearly still have deep affection for you, John. You're a wonderful man and I definitely don't want you to die in a tiger enclosure, but if the tiger is essentially forcing us be honest...

TIGER. I am.

LINDA. Okay. John, I don't love you anymore.

TIGER. Wow. Wow. So, um… I thought she was going to say she was just bored and then you'd decide to work together to get the magic back. This is not what I intended and I'm really sorry. That's my fault for being so curious.

JOHN. You know when you already know something, but it doesn't feel real until someone says it out loud?

> (**LINDA** *gets up and moves to sit next to* **JOHN**. *All three of them are in a row and look very uncomfortable.* **LINDA** *takes* **JOHN**'s *hand. They do not look at each other.*)

LINDA. I'm sorry.

TIGER. I'd offer you free passes to the zoo to make this less awkward, but I'm pretty sure you're both banned for life at this point. Who knows though, life is really long. Eventually, they'll probably forget all about this.

> (**JOHN** *and* **LINDA** *look at the* **TIGER**.)

End of Play

Good Luck Fortune Cookies

GOOD LUCK FORTUNE COOKIES premiered on October 21, 2024, at Town Hall in New York, NY, as part of The 24 Hour Plays on Broadway (Mark Armstrong, Artistic Director). The production was directed by Satya Bhabha. The cast was as follows:

AVA ....Avantika
RITA .... Margarita Leviev
SIMON .... David Burtka
"GOLDIE" ....Ari Graynor

CHARACTERS

AVA – A woman, in love with love, very gentrified Dumbo, in a long-term relationship with Rita, head over heels. Tries to keep it pleasant.

RITA – A woman, fiery temper, slightly less-gentrified Greenpoint, in a long-term relationship with Ava, but she sometimes slips and forgets.

SIMON – A businessman, upbeat and chipper, the heir to Good Luck Fortune Cookies, nice for someone whose family is dedicated to evil.

"GOLDIE" – An ageless primordial goddess, a horror not meant for this world – but still professional, she's currently "working on herself."

AUTHOR'S NOTES

[ ] in the script indicate overlapping dialogue.

You'll need: a large bowl of unwrapped fortune cookies and a big red box.

This all tumbles ahead, it's not thoughtful. They are not thinking about any of this.

(The simply-appointed lobby of the Good Luck Fortune Cookies factory. Some benches and fake plants are the only decor. Through a large glass window, we can see a fortune cookie baking/assembly line.)

*(**AVA** and **RITA** are seated on one of the benches. **AVA** is looking around, taking everything in. **RITA** looks frustrated and can't keep her foot from tapping.)*

AVA. Babe. I love you. You've got to calm down. Rita, oh my god, look at your foot.

*(**RITA** looks and then stops tapping her foot.)*

You only tap your foot like that when you're about to blow up. And like, I don't want you to blow up in the lobby of a fortune cookie factory.

RITA. I'm fine.

AVA. You're clearly not fine. We can still leave. It's like I told you twenty-seven times, it's just a stupid little fortune, it doesn't mean anything. It didn't even have lucky lottery numbers on the back.

RITA. Ava, have you lost your mind? It's the most incredibly specific and total bullshit fortune that's ever been baked into a fucking fortune cookie and I want some answers. The end.

AVA. You only think it's specific. Do you have any idea how complex a conspiracy would have to be to ensure that I got that exact fortune cookie at Brooklyn Won Ton? We hardly ever even go there.

*(Before **RITA** can respond, **SIMON** enters. He's business casual and all smiles. He's carrying a large bowl of fortune cookies. He doesn't reference them; he's just holding the bowl.)*

SIMON. Ladies, I'm so sorry to keep you waiting. It's just so rare we have visitors. But welcome, obviously. Welcome to the Good Luck Fortune Cookie factory. I'm Simon Good. My family has run this place for generations. We're the ninth-largest distributor of fortune cookies in the continental United States. But we like ninth, it works for us.

AVA. Oh wow, Simon Good. That's the "good" in Good Luck Fortune Cookies.

SIMON. That's right.

RITA. So it's not just the "good" in the phrase "Good Luck?"

SIMON. That too.

AVA. Oh my gosh, we did not mean to bother like, the actual owner.

RITA. Speak for yourself.

SIMON. Oh no, don't worry. My grandfather owns the company. I haven't slaughtered enough innocents yet to move into upper management. But I'll get there. In the meantime, I'm free to meet with our valuable customers. When they visit. Which again, doesn't happen very often.

RITA. Did you say slaughtered [enough –?]

AVA. [Okay, well,] it's nice to meet you, Mr. Good. I'm Ava and this is Rita, my girlfriend.

SIMON. Please, call me Simon. Mr. Good is my father. And my grandfather.

*(**AVA** and **SIMON** share a chuckle. **RITA** does not chuckle.)*

RITA. I hate to kill the mood, but we have a complaint about your product, Simon.

SIMON. Well that's no good. How can I help?

(RITA pulls a small fortune slip out of her pocket and hands it to him.)

RITA. Ava got this fortune out of one of your fortune cookies.

SIMON. "You are meant to be happy in love with another. Just not Rita."

RITA. "You are meant to be happy in love with another. Just not Rita." Please explain to me how this bizarre fortune that name checks me is inside a random cookie that my girlfriend opened?

AVA. I'm, uh, sure it's a simple misunderstanding. Right, Mr. Good?

SIMON. Please, call me Simon. Mr. Good is my father. And my grandfather. Now Rita, did you also open one of our cookies?

RITA. Mine just said, "Never forget kindness."

SIMON. Oh, that's a good one. You got a good one. But I can tell by the look on your face that it's not helping. So to answer your question, let's try a little experiment.

(He holds out the bowl. Thank God, he's been holding it this whole time.)

Please, each of you – take another cookie. On the house.

(They do. And they both crack them open, take out the fortunes, and read.)

RITA. "Attitude is a little thing that makes a big difference." Okay, fuck this cookie too.

AVA. "You are meant to be happy..." Oh no.

(RITA grabs the fortune from AVA and reads.)

RITA. "You are meant to be happy in love with another. Just not Rita." This is un-fucking-believable!

AVA. Honey, please don't get mad. I'm sure there's an explanation and after we get it, we can go to dinner at 21 Greenpoint and have that cheeseburger you love that used to be off-menu but now is on the printed menu, okay?

RITA. Simon? Thoughts? We came all the way out here; we took a fucking boat to the middle of nowhere to get some answers.

SIMON. We're on Staten Island.

RITA. Why is this happening?!

AVA. It does seem more unusual now.

SIMON. I think you should both try again.

(AVA talks another cookie. RITA takes three and quickly opens them, letting the pieces of cookie fall on the ground. AVA opens her cookie as well.)

RITA. "A journey of a thousand miles begins with a single step."

"Goodness is the only investment that never fails."

"Always do the right thing and you will be happy."

AVA. "You are meant to be happy in love with another. Just not Rita."

SIMON. Ava, is there a reason you maybe shouldn't be with Rita?

RITA. Hey. Fuck you, pal.

SIMON. Well, normally I'd just say, "Oh well, another day in the skinning room." But there's only one explanation at this point. It looks like Ava's caught the attention of our Chief Content Officer.

AVA. The skinning room?

SIMON. Oh no, it just sounds bad. It's really just a small room where people are skinned alive. It's funny, as it happens, I'm a something of an amateur chef and sometimes for family dinner I'll take the scraps from the skinning [room floor and –]

AVA. [Rita, I think we] should go. I love you, isn't that enough? Let's leave here now.

RITA. I'm not leaving because he tried to scare us by saying some creepy shit in a too-nice-voice. Who is this Chief Content Officer? Your Grandfather? You said he's in charge, right?

SIMON. Oh no, silly. My Grandfather can barely hold a pen anymore. He's sort of a figurehead.

(A pleasant chime sounds.)

That's not good.

AVA. That lovely chime's not good?

RITA. It didn't sound bad.

(A pleasant chime sounds again.)

SIMON. Looks like you might get your wish. Sounds like the Chief Content Officer is coming down. This is very rare. So quickly, just one thing: Don't make her mad. She has a temper. I mean, she's working on it, she's definitely on a journey of personal growth. But don't make her mad.

RITA. And what's her name?

SIMON. Golgoth the Dreaming Mother of Future Screams, She Who Should Never Be Awakened.

RITA. I'm sorry, what?

SIMON. Golgoth the Dreaming Mother of Future Screams, She Who Should Never Be Awakened. I know, it's a real mouthful. You can call her "Goldie." Everyone around here does and it's mostly fine.

AVA. Mostly?

(A pleasant chime sounds again.)

SIMON. That's three. Here she comes.

*("**GOLDIE**" enters. She's very put together in a skirt, blouse, and heels. All office appropriate, but still chic. She's carrying a big red box. Honestly, she looks really fucking cool. Both **WOMEN** are floored. She hands the box to **SIMON**. He holds the big box in one hand and the bowl of fortune cookies in the other.)*

"GOLDIE". It took me a minute to get down here. I understand there's a problem with your fortune.

RITA. We, um, we were just explaining to Mr. Good [that…]

SIMON. [Please, call] me Simon. Mr. Good is my father. And my grandfather.

"GOLDIE". You sound silly when you say that, Simon. Your father and grandfather are also named Simon.

RITA. Why would you all have the same name?

*(Suddenly, **"GOLDIE"** screams! It's horrifying and sharp.)*

"GOLDIE". Sorry. That's just a thing I do. Anyway, the name thing is my fault. I make every male born into the Good family take the name Simon. It's just easier to remember after generations of being in a blood pact to bring their company success while also quietly plotting the end of humanity and a return to chaos, you know? I'm all about simplicity lately. It's part of my ongoing journey of personal growth. I'm working on myself.

AVA. You, um, excuse me. You made a blood pact with the owners of a fortune cookie company?

"GOLDIE". Yes. You're very attractive. Anyway, I made a blood pact with the Good family. Look, I don't get to pick who awakens me by summoning my essence from the unknowable hellscape dimension where I was sleeping. It's right there in the name, "Golgoth the Dreaming Mother of Future Screams, She Who Should Never Be Awakened." They awakened me anyway. So what am I going to do? Oh, you can just call me "Goldie." I feel like that will go okay.

RITA. And – and we're supposed to believe you're, what? A demon?

AVA. I believe it.

"GOLDIE". Rita does, too. Don't you, Rita? And actually, I'm a primordial goddess. Sowing chaos, ruining lives, all that. Need more proof, Rita? Okay, Ava keeps getting the same fortune cookie fortune over and over because you've cheated on the poor girl so many times that it's hard for me to keep count. And I've been around for a long time. And Ava kind of knows, but she actively decides to "not know" because she loves you, but that just makes it worse.

> (**RITA** *was not ready for that.* **AVA** *just looks down.*)

RITA. That's – that's so – crazy.

"GOLDIE". And Ava didn't want to come here today because she knew, somewhere way down deep in her heart, that this would all probably be dragged to the surface. But I mean, she couldn't have guessed the primordial goddess part. Honestly, it would be unfair to think she could ever guess the primordial goddess part.

> (*Suddenly,* **"GOLDIE"** *screams! It's horrifying and sharp.*)

RITA. Ava, this is bullshit. You don't believe her, do you, Ava?

AVA. No. No, I don't believe her.

"GOLDIE". Fuck, you are so sweet. I hate to do this, but a short list would include Alison, Brie, Charmaine, Patty, Linda from SoulCycle, Elise, Charmaine again, Daphne, and Jan.

*(We see this land on **AVA**. Meanwhile –)*

RITA. Big fucking deal, "Goldie." Big fucking list of female names. What does any of this have to do with fucking Fortune Cookies?

"GOLDIE". You have a real problem with how I do my job. What exactly do you do?

RITA. That's none of your fucking business.

AVA. I'm a doctoral student in Romantic Literature at Columbia and Rita runs a dance studio.

"GOLDIE". Wow. Romantic Literature, huh? Exactly how romantic?

*(She's flirting with **AVA**. It's not subtle.)*

AVA. Very romantic.

RITA. Are you fucking kidding me? You're gonna flirt with her right in front of my face.

AVA. You were the one who wanted to come here. Be careful what you wish for. And flirting with her is better than sleeping with other women behind your back. Women like Charmaine. Twice. And since apparently we're less committed than I thought, I've got some room to maneuver.

RITA. You're "maneuvering" with a monster.

AVA, "GOLDIE" & SIMON. Whoa!

SIMON. I'm afraid I'll have to cut your tongue out if you insult her again.

AVA. Honestly, Rita. Have a little bit of tact. She just told us she's on a journey of personal growth.

RITA. Ava, what? Okay, this is insane. I'm literally going insane.

>*(Suddenly, "**GOLDIE**" screams! It's horrifying and sharp. It really is bone chilling.)*

"GOLDIE". Again, my fault. It just happens. Anyway ladies, I brought this special box down with me and I think it will clear everything up. It's the quickest way to cut through all the chatter. It's a secret box from my secret collection. Would you like to know its secret name?

RITA. [Not at all.]

AVA. [No, thank you.]

"GOLDIE". Fine. Your loss. Anyway, it will show you your future and you'll see if you really belong together.

SIMON. This is exciting. She doesn't usually do this.

>*(**AVA** takes the box from **SIMON**. **RITA** takes one side of it.)*

AVA. What if we don't like what it shows us?

RITA. Or what if it's another weird fucked-up trick?

"GOLDIE". Hey, I don't mean to interrupt but listen. I might be Golgoth the Dreaming Mother of Future Screams, She Who Should Never Be Awakened, but I'm not a total dick. Just think of it like a big, red fortune cookie. And I've got discord to sow and a lunch meeting, so tick tock.

AVA. I think I want to look. Seems to be kind of a lot of stuff I don't know.

RITA. Whatever. Let's just get this over with.

*(They open it together. Everything plunges into blackness as a strobe light illuminates the stage and a deafening roar fills the space! And I mean as loud as fucking possible. **RITA** and **AVA** collapse to the ground dead! The strobe and roar stop, and lights restore.)*

*(Pause. **SIMON** gently prods **RITA** with his foot. She doesn't move.)*

"GOLDIE". Huh. Guess it was the wrong box.

End of Play

I Buried Doug Biggers Alive but He's Probably Dead by Now

I BURIED DOUG BIGGERS ALIVE BUT HE'S PROBABLY DEAD BY NOW premiered on June 2, 2016, as a part of the 21st Summer Shorts Festival at Carnival Studio Theatre, Adrienne Arsht Center for the Performing Arts. It was commissioned by City Theatre (Magaret Ledford, Artistic Director) in Miami, FL. The production was directed Paul Tei. The cast was as follows:

DIANE BIGGERS . . . . Elizabeth Dimon
MAX HUMMEL . . . . Alex Alvarez
CINDY EK . . . . Karen Stephens
AMBER MILLS . . . . .Meredith Bartmon
JIM CHIRP . . . . Andres Maldonado
BABS CHIRP. . . . . .Cherise James
FLIP BARNES . . . . Tom Wahl

CHARACTERS

DIANE BIGGERS – a woman, a wife, no nonsense, matter of fact, charming proof that enough can be enough

MAX HUMMEL – a gravedigger by trade

CINDY EK – a home improvement store employee

AMBER MILLS – a customer at the home improvement store

JIM CHIRP – a married amateur entomologist

BABS CHIRP – a married amateur entomologist

FLIP BARNES – a popular local meteorologist

AUTHOR'S NOTES

This all moves quickly. It's fast and fun. It's not thoughtful.

For ease of navigation, standard text is used when characters are addressing the audience and *italicized text in dialogue* indicates that characters are talking to other people onstage.

When the stuffed animals start falling, it would be ideal if there were a lot and even more ideal if they were mostly insects.

The giant flower at the end is its own thing. Good luck.

(**DIANE** *stands. There is a lone chair next to her, but she stands.*)

(*Most everyone else is scattered around, too. Looking at us.* **FLIP** *in a suit.* **CINDY** *is in jeans, a short sleeve polo shirt, and a uniform mono-colored apron.* **JIM** *and* **BABS** *stand together in different shades of brown and khaki. They're a package deal. She's holding something like a butterfly net. He's holding a book in one hand and a stuffed butterfly under his arm.* **MAX** *is grim and has a shovel.* **AMBER** *is not onstage yet. She's shopping.*)

(*There is a pile of dirt onstage. It's not a mound, just roughly the size and length of a freshly-covered grave. It has its own area, like any other character.*)

DIANE. Fun story: I buried Doug Biggers alive. But he's probably dead by now. He always had to have the last word, but not this time. Oh, a bit of context, Doug Biggers was my husband. And you're probably thinking to yourselves, "That Diane is such a joker." I'm Diane. Hello. And if you are thinking I'm a joker then you're mistaken. I'm being absolutely frank with you. This is a kind of confession for posterity. Well, it's more of an explanation as to why my husband deserved to be buried alive, which he did, but I'm not going to sit here and parse words, we just met.

Now, just a factual note right at the beginning: I can't take all of the credit. I'm not the best with a shovel. So while I did drug his nightly Campari and soda, haul his overstuffed body to the car, purchase all the materials and build the pine box myself, I had to pay a sort of dark and gloomy man that hangs out near the local Piggly Wiggly to dig the actual hole.

MAX. I'm Max Hummel.

DIANE. And then I nailed the lid onto a pine box, pushed it into the ground, that was difficult because Max said he was only there to dig the hole and didn't want to be an "accessory" to anything.

MAX. Me again.

DIANE. Yes. *Bad news, Max. You're an accessory.* So then I paid him to fill in the hole again with my unconscious husband on the business end of the dirt.

MAX. I used this shovel.

DIANE. Just to go back for a second: my husband did have a Campari and soda every night. It's like drinking watered down battery acid, so bitter.

MAX. I enjoy a Campari and soda.

DIANE. *Oh shut up, Max.* He also used to click his fork against his teeth when he would eat. His fork. Imagine that sound right now. Now multiply it over many, many, many years. He also used my toothbrush because in his mind toothbrushes are interchangeable, which they are not. And listen, I wish I could tell you this all happened a long time ago because distance makes things more comfortable. But the fact is I buried him last night. So there is a world where he's still somehow struggling for air, barely hanging in, but honestly he was never a very optimistic person, so I imagine he's given up by now and simply died.

CINDY. I'm Cindy Ek.

DIANE. This is Cindy. We've become fast friends. She sold me the pinewood at the local home improvement store and has been a tremendous resource.

CINDY. *Thanks, Diane.* Pine is actually our most commonly purchased soft wood for building projects, so I didn't really do anything that special.

DIANE. She offered me the use of her table saw to facilitate building the casket.

CINDY. I keep my workshop at home very clean. That matters with pine because it dents easily. And the last thing you want is to have to sand things out.

DIANE. It was sweet of her to worry, but I didn't care about dents and scratches because I was building a coffin to imprison my husband after years of verbal abuse, criticism, and casual cruelty. It was going in the ground.

CINDY. Now I belong to a support group for survivors of domestic violence, so I really understood what Diane was going through. She was very candid about the level of verbal abuse.

DIANE. People can be mean. But the fork on the teeth thing? Absolutely not.

CINDY. I sort of thought "burying him alive" was just a symbolic exercise at first so she could get up the strength to leave.

DIANE. No, I killed him. Well, I prefer to think suffocation killed him. Or is killing him. I just built the box and provided helpful access to said box.

>   (**AMBER** *enters the scene. She might be pushing a shopping cart or carrying a shopping basket. She might have only a purse.*)

CINDY. Part of me felt like I should try to discourage Diane. She seemed so nice and nice people don't usually kill people. But she really won me over.

AMBER. *Excuse me, but do you work here? I'm trying to find the light bulbs.*

> *(Everyone looks at **AMBER**. **CINDY** tries not to acknowledge her.)*

CINDY. *I'll be with you in just a moment, ma'am.*

AMBER. *Can you just point? I only need the light bulbs.*

CINDY. *I'm in the middle of something here.*

> *(She points to the audience. **AMBER** sees them.)*

AMBER. *Oh! Oh, my gosh.*

CINDY. *What is your name?*

AMBER. *Amber Mills.*

CINDY. *Well, Amber, you're in the show now. So just hold on a second.*

> *(**AMBER** sort of poses, taking the audience in. It's as if perhaps she's the new star of the show. But she's not. **DIANE** is the star.)*

DIANE. Now, in addition to always needing the last word, using my toothbrush, and generally being a mean person, the details of which could melt paint, my perhaps almost late husband also illegally imported strange "herbal remedies" from China. In case you're feeling sorry for him, just know that you've been paying his tax burden for years.

JIM. I'm Jim.

BABS. I'm Babs. We're the Chirps.

JIM. That's our last name.

BABS. *How was what I said not clear?*

JIM. *Maybe they think being a Chirp is a profession.*

BABS. *It does feels like work sometimes.*

JIM. We're entomologists.

BABS. Amateur entomologists. This isn't really a butterfly net, it's for fishing. Or pool cleaning. Real butterfly nets are expensive. We have a mortgage.

DIANE. Jim and Babs are in my book club. Between us, their attitudes and opinions about the reading selections can be a little bit pedestrian.

JIM. *We can hear you.*

DIANE. Regardless, I hired them to explain my hopefully expired husband's illegal product of choice as I don't particularly like talking about it.

BABS. *Ophiocordyceps sinensis* is a fungus that germinates in the living larva of the Ghost Moth. It kills and mummifies the little larva and then a stalk-like "fruiting body" emerges from the corpse, like a little flower springing from the grave.

DIANE. It's pretty dark.

BABS. Oh, but its regional name Yartsa Gunbu means, "winter worm, summer grass." That takes the edge off the "fruiting body" in a corpse thing.

JIM. That "fruiting body" is known in English colloquially as caterpillar fungus and has been used for two thousand years, mostly to remedy erectile dysfunction.

CINDY. *Oh wow.*

AMBER. *What kind of show is this?*

DIANE. *It's my show, Amber, please be quiet.*

BABS. The Ghost Moth is endangered now due to overharvesting. This "fruiting body" grows primarily in mountainous regions of India, Nepal, and Tibet. People spend entire lives searching hillsides to farm it. That sounds so romantic. Not the erectile dysfunction part, but the lovely hillsides part.

DIANE. This is all true, by the way. And have you noticed how they keep putting air quotes around the phrase "fruiting body" like it's not the right phrase? Honestly, I'm not a fan of their energy. They have an odd energy.

JIM. *We really can hear you.*

DIANE. *You have an odd energy. I don't like it.*

BABS. *She's right, Jim. You have an odd energy. It's off-putting.*

JIM. *She said both of us.*

BABS. *I'm full of interesting skills and abilities that you know nothing about, Jim. You'd be filled with wonder. So she one hundred percent means you.*

JIM. *Did you mean just me?*

BABS. *This is why I want that divorce.*

JIM. *Babs, we agreed not to talk about this in front of people.*

BABS. *We also agreed you wouldn't have your stuffed animal collection in public.* While I was initially shocked over what Diane had done, it really got me thinking about my own marriage.

JIM. We're considering a trial separation.

BABS. *Whatever you need to tell yourself, Jim.*

MAX. *Hey.*

BABS. *Oh. Hi.*

DIANE. Now you'd think importing illegal insect erectile dysfunction fungus, indulging in cruelty, and always needing to be right are all bad enough. And being a very loud mouth breather. You know the kind, just always breathing. But my hopefully-deceased-soon husband was also a cheater.

FLIP. I'm Flip Barnes.

DIANE. *And no one is getting out of this with clean hands.*

FLIP. Oh God.

DIANE. I spent a fair amount of time imagining the person my husband might have an affair with.

BABS. And almost every book in that depressing book club.

DIANE. *Yes. Thank you, Babs, exactly.* Based on all of that, I just assumed any cheating would be with a younger woman. I had prepared myself for the fact that a man handling endangered dead caterpillar erectile dysfunction drugs may possibly be seeing someone on the side.

FLIP. It was just a few dinners.

DIANE. Then I discovered, quite by accident, it was a popular local meteorologist.

FLIP. She went through his phone.

DIANE. I accidentally went through his phone.

FLIP. She found a very private picture I sent Doug.

CINDY. *Can I see it?*

DIANE. *Not now, Cindy.*

FLIP. *It wasn't for you.*

DIANE. *The notion of the statement, "It wasn't for you." gets very slippery when you're talking about you sending explicit pictures to a married man.*

>   (**FLIP** *takes a step forward and a special warmly illuminates him. Maybe there's even scoring to this.*[*] **DIANE** *looks annoyed.*)

---

[*] A license to produce *I Buried Doug Biggers Alive but He's Probably Dead by Now* does not include a performance license for any third-party or copyrighted music. Licensees should create an original composition or use music in the public domain. For further information, please see the Music and Third-Party Materials Use Note on page iii.

FLIP. A friend recommended Doug because I was going through a crisis of confidence. It's difficult being a meteorologist because you're wrong a lot and no matter how perfect your smile or nice your suit, people start to resent you. And I have a great smile. But being less than reliable on a nightly basis gets in your head, undermines your confidence. And it started affecting my "prowess." It really threw me for a loop. I was essentially becoming an unreliable Doppler radar prediction in bed. Which is really a poor metaphor anyway, as meteorologists use a pulse-Doppler technique as just one piece of an accurate weather forecast but an erection is sort of the primary tool in sexual gratification.

CINDY. *You're losing the thread a little bit, Flip.*

FLIP. *Right. Yes.* So Doug sold me some of his caterpillar fungus and two thousand years of Chinese medicine isn't wrong. Worked like a charm. And he was so supportive and eager to experience the results first hand. He said it was part of ensuring quality control.

*(**DIANE** snaps and his special light disappears. He steps back.)*

DIANE. It's like the opening of a really unfortunate pornographic film.

AMBER. *Oh no. I'm just going to ask again, what kind of show is this?*

DIANE. *Get out of here, Amber! Get out of here right now!*

*(**AMBER** leaves. Reluctantly. As she goes, **CINDY** whispers after her...)*

CINDY. *Light bulbs are on aisle eleven.*

DIANE. The point is, no matter the gender or nature of the affair, my soon-if-not-already-dead husband betrayed me.

MAX. *I don't see what's so wrong with a harmless affair. Do you, Babs?*

BABS. If your marriage is ending, for instance. And a mysterious stranger appeared offering a brief escape from the realities of your everyday life. It would be better than burying someone alive, I suppose.

MAX. *Hey.*

BABS. *Hi.*

JIM. *Can you please not be so overt?*

BABS. *I said "Hi."*

JIM. *The depth of meaning in that, "Hi," wasn't lost on anyone here.*

BABS. *Okay. I'm going to leave you now to drown in your stuffed animals, Jim.*

> *(She leaves **JIM**'s side and goes to stand next to **MAX**.)*

JIM. *Seriously?!*

BABS. *Drown in your stupid stuffed animals, Jim!*

JIM. *Stop saying that.*

BABS. *Drown in them!! Drown in them!!*

> *(Suddenly the lights flicker and dozens upon dozens of stuffed animals start falling from the sky but only above **JIM**. They crash down and accumulate. Well, they don't crash because they're stuffed animals, but they gently pelt him. This goes on for a while. It's a lot of stuffed animals. **BABS** is delighted. It finally stops.)*

I told him that he'd be "filled with wonder."

DIANE. This. This is the odd energy I was talking about. Although, it does make me feel validated to inspire other women to stand up for themselves. If I had done that sooner, maybe it wouldn't haven't come to this.

FLIP. *Yes! You see that? You could have done that. Well, not the weird stuffed animal thing, but you could have left Doug anytime. Just like Babs is leaving Jim. Sorry, Jim. You didn't have to stick around, suffer, and then completely go overboard by burying him alive.*

DIANE. *Well, I suppose we all handle things in our own way, Flip. You eat parasitic fungus and sleep with married men. I rely on passive homicide.*

FLIP. *It's not exactly equivalent.* No matter what she says, even if all of it is true, Doug was nice to me. He was special. And I miss him.

> (**FLIP** *is genuinely heartbroken.* **DIANE** *takes him in.*)

DIANE. Please don't cry. This all sounds terrible. I sound terrible; I know it. I just don't feel bad. But then, that's...

> (*Pause. She sits down in the chair for the first time.*)

That's not entirely true. All of this is an effort to not feel bad. I never thought I was the kind of person who might regret something, but the very appealing fantasy of burying your husband alive after years of bullshit, abuse, cheating, little flowers growing out of zombie caterpillar bodies to help with erections, that fantasy of burying him alive is much different than actually doing it. I do feel bad, I do. What was I thinking? Honestly, if Doug Biggers had been redeemable in even a tiny way none of this would have happened. I wanted him to be worthwhile; you have to believe me. I just needed one moment of kindness, one lovely thing.

(The pile of dirt begins to shift a bit. Everyone looks. An enormous [or at least very large] flower bursts out of one end of the dirt, just like a "fruiting body" out of a caterpillar larva. It's surreal and maybe even a little disturbing. It's also one lovely thing.)

*(**DIANE** shakes her head and chuckles.)*

End of Play

Music for an Abandoned Zoo

MUSIC FOR AN ABANDONED ZOO was created for The 24 Hour Plays Los Angeles Online (Mark Armstrong, Artistic Director). The production was directed by Jaki Bradley. The cast was as follows:

AMY..Pauline Chalamet
TIM..Matthew Morrison

CHARACTERS

AMY
TIM

MUSIC NOTE

A license to produce *Music for an Abandoned Zoo* does not include a performance license for any third-party or copyrighted music. Licensees should create an original composition or use music in the public domain. For further information, please see the Music and Third-Party Materials Use Note on page iii.

(The old Los Angeles Zoo in Griffith Park. Now an abandoned "Lonely Planet" tourist spot and frequent target of graffiti. **AMY** *and* **TIM** *stand by one of the large, empty exhibit habitats. Notably, they each have a ukulele. A tin can sits on the ground in front of them.)*

(This should all clip along until it suddenly doesn't.)

AMY. There are people.

TIM. Amy, where?

AMY. Whatever. There are a few people anyway, are you gonna play something?

*(**TIM** starts to play a little tune but abruptly stops.)*

TIM. I'm nervous. If nobody puts money in the tin can, does that mean we screwed up the whole, like, memorial thing?

AMY. I don't think it really matters.

TIM. It matters.

AMY. And I'm saying, Tim, that it really doesn't. Now that we're here, it doesn't.

*(**TIM** plucks a few notes. Nope.)*

TIM. This place makes me sad. Like is it full of all the spirits of animals who died here?

AMY. Animal ghosts?

TIM. Maybe. If they died here, I'm sure it wasn't their favorite place.

AMY. It was a city zoo, not an Eastern European gulag. And now it's a park. Jesus, Tim.

TIM. I'm just uncomfortable, okay? Like I actively don't want to be here.

AMY. And yet we're here.

TIM. And I'm looking around thinking this is a fucked-up place to bring kids and teach them to play the ukulele. For money. So, like, people in the park would put quarters in a can or whatever. So yeah, it's fucked up that Mom used to bring us here.

AMY. She's dead. It's actually fucked up that we came back here now that she's dead.

TIM. Wow. Okay, Amy. Just go right for it, huh?

(Honestly, **AMY** *is a little gobsmacked.)*

AMY. What? She's dead? Cancer, headscarf, Fentanyl lollipops, a funeral, sound familiar? Or I'm sorry, is it unclear that she's dead?

TIM. No.

AMY. Are you sure, because you seem shocked?

TIM. No.

AMY. Because last March on a Tuesday you put her ashes into her favorite ukulele and pushed it out to fucking sea and lit a candle or some shit. And I only remember the day because I had to work and you did it anyway without me.

TIM. She was in a plastic bag in a box in the kitchen and you kept making excuses.

AMY. A job is not an excuse, Tim. A job is what normal adults go to so they can earn money and pay for things.

A sister is what people like you lean on because they have no job.

TIM. Finding a job isn't easy, okay?

AMY. But somehow I have a job. And mom had a job. Mom was dying and she had a job.

TIM. Fuck.

AMY. In fact, look around and almost everyone else we both know has a job they have to go to every day. Did we all just get really lucky? Is that it?

TIM. Got it. So I'm a lazy, selfish piece of shit and now she's gone. I said goodbye and sent her out into the water, and you missed it. So I'm awful. What now?

AMY. You got to say goodbye. I didn't. Think about that.

TIM. You were never gonna do it.

AMY. Sorry I wasn't processing her death on your timetable.

TIM. That's not what I'm saying.

AMY. Grieving is different for everyone and you left me in the dust.

TIM. You seem to be doing just fine with it now.

AMY. Oh, fuck off or I will punch in the fucking mouth.

TIM. Okay, let's earn some money, right? Show me how it's done. Play something.

AMY. Fuck. Off.

TIM. No, do it now. Play something now and say goodbye. Play something for some spare change from strangers like we did when we were kids. Play the god damned ukulele for mom and all the dead animal ghosts, Amy.

(She doesn't.)

Fucking play it!!

(She still doesn't. Suddenly, she kicks the tin can away with a shout!)

(They both stand there for a minute. Grief is different things for different people and that's what we're watching right now. Then...)

AMY. She never even cared about the spare change.

TIM. She cared about it when it was time to buy peppermint schnapps.

AMY. The peppermint schnapps.

TIM. And she'd give us each a little sip.

AMY. But I do think she just loved hearing us play.

TIM. You think?

AMY. I really do.

TIM. I guess maybe because it's the only thing she could ever make us do together.

(Fuck. **AMY** *looks like she has more to say, but she stops herself. She basically bites back her realization. Instead she sets down her ukulele.)*

AMY. Just...yeah, this was stupid. I'll just leave this here. With all the other ghosts.

TIM. Why? We're doing the memorial thing. Don't leave. Look, I'm sorry I yelled.

AMY. Don't be sorry.

(She starts to go.)

TIM. Okay. I guess I'll talk to you later then.

AMY. Sure, maybe.

(And she's gone.)

*(**TIM** plucks a few more notes. Then he suddenly plays an entire little tune for the ghosts of the dead animals. Maybe the tune for his mom.)*

End of Play

A Mysterious Horse

A MYSTERIOUS HORSE was created for The 24 Hour Plays Viral Monologues (Mark Armstrong, Artistic Director). It premiered in Round 13 on June 23, 2020. The cast was as follows:

BRENDA . . . . .Zosia Mamet

CHARACTERS

BRENDA

(**BRENDA** *starts recording on her cell phone camera. She is in a bathroom with the door closed. She's still in pajamas. And she looks pretty freaked out. She has a toothbrush hanging out of her mouth, but after a moment she suddenly remembers it's there. This is all frantic and paced up!*)

(*There is a real sense of dread under everything, even if it's ridiculous.*)

BRENDA. Janine! Janine, oh my god. It's Brenda, that's so stupid you can see me. Janine, I'm sending you a video because I was brushing my teeth just now, fuck –

(*She takes out the toothbrush but keeps it in her hand.*)

I know we haven't talked in a while, I know that's my fault, but I hope to god you watch this. So just now, I just happened to glance out the bedroom window and, okay, I'm upstate right now, and I looked outside and there's just a horse standing in my yard and it's not my horse, Janine. And I'm like why is there a horse outside? It's not moving. It's very still, like an ominous kind of still. Shit, I just realized I probably look like a seventy-year-old man in Boca Raton, but these are my favorite pajamas, Janine, and it's still morning here and there's some strange horse outside. And, okay I know how this sounds, but I just...

(*She opens the door and peeks out, then closes it again. She then leans in close...*)

It was staring up at me. Staring like it could see me in the upstairs window.

(She is dead serious.)

God, it gave me chills. I mean it's a plain brown horse. It doesn't have, like, I don't know, red flaming eyes or anything. It's not menacing. It is menacing, but not traditionally menacing. But it stared at me so I kind of ducked behind the curtains. And when I pulled the curtain back a little and looked again, the horse was walking towards the house, up towards the front door. And I'm thinking what the fuck is wrong with this spooky horse? Like what is this horse's problem? But Janine –

(She is interrupted by a banging and a thud from somewhere in the house. She looks around, terrified, waiting for more noises. Breathing faster, she places her hand on the door, bracing it. She turns to the camera and whispers...)

The horse is in the house.

(She laughs at herself, but it's not funny. She's genuinely afraid. This is getting into horror movie territory.)

It sounds insane, but that horse is in the house and I heard it come up the stairs, Janine. And I don't know what it wants and I don't want to know, but it wants something, Janine. It wants something from me. And I really think it might hurt me or do something even worse. I love horses, you know I love horses more than anything, but this horse is up to no good. This horse is dangerous. So I'm hiding here and thinking what could it possibly want? And then...then I thought of you.

And I'm recording this video for you and texting a copy of it to everyone down at the stables because I know, Janine. I have no idea how, but I'd bet money that you sent this horse to terrify me, possibly even kill me. Didn't you? Didn't you, Janine?!

(She catches herself being loud and gets quieter again.)

Fuck. You don't have to answer. Who else but you would train a horse to stalk people? Who else but you would teach a horse how to commit a home invasion? So let me be super clear here, all right?

I am sorry that you think I stole your place in the barn.

I am sorry that I humiliated you at the Adirondack Horse show.

I am sorry that I sent a sympathy flower arrangement to your home you lost.

That was unkind. It was not a nice thing to do. So if I survive this insane thing, I will apologize in person. But if this horse murders me here in the bathroom in my own home, Janine, everyone at the stables will have this video. Everyone will all know you were behind this brutal attack.

(Two swift bangs on the door! **BRENDA** *screams and drops the toothbrush! Things are totally crazy now! She is freaking out! She grabs her phone!)*

Oh my god, oh my god, please no! Go away, horse! Go away!!

(The lights crash to black as she screams!)

End of Play

She Said Everything's Moving Faster

SHE SAID EVERYTHING'S MOVING FASTER was created for The 24 Hour Plays Viral Monologues (Mark Armstrong, Artistic Director). It premiered in Round 37 on March 15, 2022. The cast was as follows:

NICOLE..Allison Tolman

CHARACTERS

NICOLE

(**NICOLE** *looks anxious, maybe a little manic. She is definitely manic. She's at a table in her apartment holding a bag of frozen peas or an ice pack against her cheek. It's wrapped in a black bandana.* **NICOLE**'s *jaw hurts. Also, she is notably missing a tooth.)*

(She has her phone set up on a little stand or leaning against a book. She's recording something. Maybe the video image from her phone is projected onstage.)

NICOLE. Okay, it's not as bad as it looks. My mouth stopped bleeding. This happened last night, but I walked home from the bar. It is not close. I finally got home just now and I have to tell you guys about it. Or when you see this later, whatever.

> *(**NICOLE** puts down the frozen peas or ice pack.)*

So I was walking home from the bar, bleeding from the mouth. Okay, wait. Let me start at the bar. I want this to make sense so you can please tell me I'm not crazy.

You know the bar out on Route 7 in Janesville? Good, that's where I was. I don't usually go to Janesville, but Jimmy goes to the bar here in town and I didn't want to run into him. You can scroll back a few entries to see how Jimmy cheated on me, ripped my fucking heart out, and left it on the floor to die of exposure. Sound dramatic? It's not. He's a piece of shit. And he's the reason I was at a bar in Janesville. Having a drink by myself, minding my own business, whatever. And there was this woman in a yellow raincoat by the window. Just staring out the window. Alone. She looked like the umbrella girl on a Morton's Salt container, only older. And I thought, "What the fuck?" You know? No one ever just goes up and talks to people anymore and I didn't know anyone in the bar and she was sitting there staring out the window. So walked up to her and said, "Do you mind if I sit down?"

That's it. I need to stress this, *that's all I said.*

And she – and she turned with these wild eyes, punched me in the mouth, and screamed, *"Everything's moving faster!"* And then she ran out of the bar. I fully lost a tooth. She knocked my tooth out. And I chased her. I ran down the street, but she was faster. And as she disappeared out of sight, I got dizzy, so I stopped and sat down against a wall. And then all at once I remembered –

(This all goes faster and faster.)

I saw on the news that a woman burned down her house with her husband and two children inside because she suspected he was having an affair.

I saw on the news that three women in the area have been sexually assaulted and beaten with a bat and authorities are "actively following up on leads."

I saw on the news that the company that makes my anxiety medication is being sued because several people have died after it caused an inability to swallow.

I saw on the news that the bodies of four people were found in an incinerator in the basement of a local factory after the night manager was fired.

I saw on the news that they found a mountain of dead bodies in a small Georgia town because a funeral director wanted to save money on cremation.

I saw on the news that a married couple was keeping four women imprisoned in their basement for fifteen years and the neighbors said they didn't notice.

I saw on the news that a woman lost a tooth and put it inside a Russian nesting doll and put that doll in another doll and put that doll in another doll *and put that doll into another doll and put that doll into another doll and it just kept going.*

I saw on the news that fishing boats full of dead bodies are washing ashore on the coasts of Japan and no one knows where they're coming from.

Where are they coming from? *Where the actual fuck are the boats full of dead people coming from?* It's all I could think about when I walked home. I left my car and walked from Janesville. I didn't think about Jimmy and how he broke my heart a single time. Is this an existential crisis?

Some lady punched me and now I'm either going to step in front of a moving train or live a happy life full of laughter now. *Which one?* I don't know which one.

> *(She really doesn't know which one is going to happen.)*

End of Play

Telephones & Bad Weather

TELEPHONES & BAD WEATHER premiered on May 30, 2019, as a part of the 24th Summer Shorts Festival at Carnival Studio Theatre, Adrienne Arsht Center for the Performing Arts. It was commissioned by City Theatre (Margaret Ledford, Artistic Director) in Miami, FL. The production was directed by Andy Quiroga. The cast was as follows:

LAVERNE . . . . Hannah Richter
ELISE . . . . Lindsay Corey
SCOTT. . . . . Gregg Weiner
DISCIPLES . . . . .Katherine Berger, Theresa Callion,
Natalia Quintero-Riestra & Zye Reid

CHARACTERS

LAVERNE – a pleasant but very confused neighbor

ELISE – a wife, wired, frazzled, barely holding it together

SCOTT – a husband, relentlessly positive & confident

DISCIPLES – a group of "true believers" (doomsday cultists) who are way too excited about climate change

BOOMING VOICE – a mysterious caller with a lot of instructions

AUTHOR'S NOTES

This all moves very quickly. It's fast and fun. It's not thoughtful.

When the **BOOMING VOICE** speaks on the rotary telephone, it is terrifyingly loud and broadcast through all speakers in the theatre.

The National Weather Service (US) describes moderate flooding as involving some inundation of structures and roads near streams, with some evacuations; major flooding involves extensive inundation of structures and roads and significant evacuations.

*(A suburban living room with a very aggressive thunderstorm raging outside. Everything else is pretty normal except for the small group of **DISCIPLES** to one side, all in what looks like child's pose. They are fully surrounded by dozens of kitchen glasses and plastic cups. Various sizes, but all full of water. They quietly hum a steady tone.)*

(Suddenly there is a violent knocking on the front door.)

*(**ELISE** enters the living room heading towards the door. She stops, looks at the group of **DISCIPLES**, and sighs. She shouts at them.)*

ELISE. This is a living room!

(She claps twice succinctly to get their attention.)

A living room!

*(Nothing. She continues over and opens the door. Lighting cracks as **LAVERNEE** charges inside. She has a wet raincoat on and she's carrying something bundled up in a towel.)*

LAVERNE. Oh thank goodness you answered!

ELISE. Good grief, Laverne, get in here.

LAVERNE. It's really coming down out there. I can't remember the last time we had rain like this. I got soaked through just running over from my house and I didn't... who are, Elise, what's going on in here?

ELISE. Oh just ignore them. They were outside until it started raining.

LAVERNE. It's been raining for two weeks. These people have been in your house since then doing, what are they doing? Is that yoga? Why is there a yoga class in your living room? Honestly, that huge construction project Scott has going on in your backyard is strange enough, now this?

ELISE. Oh, you think my husband's "construction project" is strange?

LAVERNE. Well, I thought it was a very elaborate pergola, but it clearly it isn't.

ELISE. No, it isn't.

LAVERNE. And there's been a lot of talk in the neighborhood about how Scott is starting to "drift" across your property lines with the construction. I've been defending you. I've been telling people it's an avant-garde guesthouse, just so you know.

ELISE. Thank you, but let's ignore that too, all right?

LAVERNE. You have quite a list of things to ignore.

ELISE. Just the two things. Now why on Earth are you out in this mess?

LAVERNE. Because I need you to take this back.

> (**LAVERNE** *removes the towel to reveal a sherbet-colored 1980s rotary dial phone. She holds it out for* **ELISE** *to take. It's clear* **ELISE** *is not going to take it. Instead, she quickly looks toward the* **DISCIPLES**, *all still bowed down, and whispers desperately.)*

ELISE. You said you would keep it at your house for me.

LAVERNE. Well, I didn't have all of the information when I agreed to that.

ELISE. It's an old phone, what more information do you need?

LAVERNE. It keeps ringing. It won't stop ringing at all hours. The sound is disturbing. The frequency of the calls is disturbing. And the fact that it's not plugged into anything is very disturbing. So take it back.

ELISE. Laverne, I understand how this might be a little unpleasant, but we've been friends for a long time and I have never asked you for anything.

LAVERNE. Elise, we are neighbors. Right now, we're neighbors. If you want to be friends, then take your spooky phone back.

(The phone rings. **LAVERNE** *holds it out as if to say, "You see?")*

(Suddenly the **DISCIPLES** *sit up in unison. Each* **DISCIPLE** *grabs one of the glasses littered around them and splashes water in their own face. Then they all look to the sky.)*

DISCIPLES. Answer the call!

LAVERNE. What is wrong with you people?

DISCIPLES. Answer the call!

LAVERNE. No.

(The phone stops ringing. The **DISCIPLES** *all settle back into their bowing positions and begin humming again.)*

ELISE. It's so frustrating, I don't mind telling you. I'm going to have to get that rug steam cleaned when it's all said and done, I just know it.

LAVERNE. Elise, you take this phone from me.

*(**ELISE** reluctantly takes the phone.)*

ELISE. I'm sorry. All the rain started and I just thought if I got it out of the house then maybe things would calm down a little. But clearly that didn't work. And it wasn't fair of me to try to unload it on you.

LAVERNE. What does the rain have to do with it? Who are these people?

ELISE. It'll sound… all right, well, they're disciples. I suppose they are like biblical disciples.

LAVERNE. Disciples?

ELISE. That's right. Disciples of Scott.

LAVERNE. Your Scott? Your husband Scott has disciples?

ELISE. Yes, Laverne, because apparently he has been chosen by God and it's every bit as crazy as it sounds and I'm doing my very best to hold it together, but I would honestly say that our marriage is in a very complicated place right now, a very difficult, touch-and-go kind of place and the phone really isn't helping so I just thought if I could get a little break from it then I might not go insane. So there you have it.

LAVERNE. Have you…have you been drinking?

ELISE. Oh Laverne, I wish. I really do wish I were at least a little tipsy.

LAVERNE. Your husband has been chosen by God?

ELISE. So he tells me. God never speaks to me directly. He kind of calls and shouts things at Scott, ordering him around, telling him to do things.

LAVERNE. To do what, exactly?

ELISE. To build an ark.

LAVERNE. Oh come on, you expect me to believe that?

ELISE. Not even a little bit. But you asked, so I'm being honest. I'm too frazzled and emotionally exhausted to be anything but honest. Global warming is going to result in horrible flooding, among other things, and my husband has to build a boat. How do you like that?

LAVERNE. I don't, as it happens. And I don't really believe in global warming.

ELISE. Out of all this, that's the part you don't believe in? That's remarkable.

LAVERNE. I thought I saw on the news "global warming" was going to make things hotter? And we just had the worst winter on record. And if it's getting warmer, isn't it supposed to mean less water?

ELISE. Ask the people in Miami about that.

LAVERNE. I've never been to Miami.

ELISE. There's a difference between climate and weather, Laverne. Climate change is the Earth gradually getting hotter over a long period time. But the changes to weather in the short term, destructive winters, floods, extreme drought, will be quite catastrophic. I've been reading up on it. Are you sure I can't get you some tea?

(The phone starts ringing.)

Damn it.

*(Again the **DISCIPLES** sit up in unison. Each **DISCIPLE** grabs one of the glasses littered around them and splashes water in their own face. Then they all look to the sky.)*

DISCIPLES. Answer the call!

ELISE. Can I get you anything? Some tea maybe?

DISCIPLES. Answer the call!

ELISE. Fine!!

*(She answers the phone and immediately holds out the receiver towards the **DISCIPLES**. A **BOOMING VOICE** fills the entire space! It*

speaks with speed and intention, frustration and anger. **LAVERNE** *has to cover her ears. It's that loud.)*

BOOMING VOICE. I've given you free will! I've given you intellect! I've given you science! I've given you the tools to correct these grievous mistakes of global warming before it's too late! Heed my words before the floods come! They will only be the beginning!

(The call ends. **ELISE** *hangs up the phone. The* **DISCIPLES** *all settle back into the bowing positions and begin humming again.)*

LAVERNE. That was…that was…

ELISE. We really don't know. It could be God or it could just be an apocalyptic message. Oh, like in the Old Testament when God speaks through some other messenger. Like a burning bush or an angel or something. I've been reading up on that, too. And a lot of legal books. I'm considering divorce.

LAVERNE. Oh! Oh no, are you okay?

ELISE. Not at all. Don't tell Scott. He's very "dedicated" to all of this.

*(***SCOTT*** comes in from the back of the house. He's shaking out a wet umbrella. He has on dress shoes, slacks, a dress shirt with the sleeves rolled up, and a pencil behind his ear. He's also carrying a hammer.)*

SCOTT. Elise, did you happen to get to the hardware store? I'm fresh out of screws and I don't think that… Oh, Laverne. How are you doing?

LAVERNE. Oh, I'm fine, just fine. Fine. Everything's fine. I just, I just needed to bring your phone back.

*(***SCOTT*** sees the phone and lights up!)*

SCOTT. Where did you find it? We've been so worried. We looked everywhere, didn't we, Elise? I took a full day away from boat building to search.

LAVERNE. So I, uh… I took it by mistake. Silly me! I used to have one just like it?

ELISE. You don't have to do that, Laverne. I gave it to her. And I couldn't go to the hardware store because the streets are flooded and also I didn't want to.

SCOTT. You gave away the phone?

ELISE. I gave it to her because I needed a break from the ringing, from everything, and you don't want to hear that so here we are.

(The phone starts ringing.)

Perfect.

*(Again the **DISCIPLES** sit up in unison. They splash water in their own faces. Then they look to the sky.)*

DISCIPLES. Answer the call!

SCOTT. We need to have an honest talk about this.

DISCIPLES. Answer the call!

*(He answers the phone and immediately holds out the receiver towards the **DISCIPLES**. A **BOOMING VOICE** fills the entire space! It speaks with speed and intention, frustration and anger. **LAVERNE** covers her ears again.)*

BOOMING VOICE. Scott. You must build an ark from cypress wood and coat it with pitch inside and out before the floods! It must be three hundred cubits long, fifty cubits wide, and thirty cubits high for all the animals! This will be too much room for men have already killed many species! But do it anyway!

*(The call ends. **SCOTT** hangs up the phone. The **DISCIPLES** all settle back into the bowing positions and begin humming again.)*

SCOTT. I mean it's pretty clear.

LAVERNE. Does it have to be so loud?

ELISE. Okay, Scott, you want to have an honest talk about this?

LAVERNE. Oh, should I be here for this?

ELISE. You can't build a boat. And you certainly can't build a boat that big alone.

SCOTT. Then help me.

ELISE. We can't do it by ourselves either.

SCOTT. Not with that attitude. Honey, I never imagined this would happen. I'm no one special, but apparently I can make a difference. And it feels good to know that I can do that. We can do that. And I love you.

ELISE. I love you too, but that doesn't fix things. You don't know anything about boats. Especially boats that big. I don't know what a cubit is but he wants it to be a lot of cubits. You don't even have boat building clothes, or rainy weather clothes. Just look at you. Why you? Why us?

SCOTT. If not us then who? What if everyone else waits for someone else to do it?

ELISE. I don't know! But it doesn't have to be us!

SCOTT. Elise, please don't say that.

ELISE. I am saying it, I'm saying in front of God and everyone, you, Laverne, your wet disciples!! I didn't sign up for this, okay?

SCOTT. We were chosen.

ELISE. He doesn't ever talk to me, you were chosen. And you're a dentist, for God's sake. We eat out all the time because neither of us can cook, we can't even make ramen and you're supposed to build an ark?! I honestly don't think I have the strength to do this, Scott. I do not have the strength.

> *(She collapses onto the couch, distraught. The phone starts ringing. The **DISCIPLES** sit up in unison. They splash water in their own faces. Then they look to the sky.)*

> *(While this is happening, **ELISE** screams at it. **LAVERNE** sits next to her on the couch and comforts her.)*

DISCIPLES. Answer the phone!

SCOTT. I have to answer it. I'm sorry.

DISCIPLES. Answer the phone!

> *(**SCOTT** answers the phone, holding it away from his ear like the last few times. But this time there is no booming voice. He looks at it quizzically and holds it up to his ear. Then carefully...)*

SCOTT. Hello?

> *(He holds the receiver out to **ELISE**.)*

Honey, it's for you?

> *(The **DISCIPLES** gasp in unison. It's such an honor! **LAVERNE** snaps at them.)*

LAVERNE. Oh, be quiet.

> *(**SCOTT** gestures for **ELISE** to take it.)*

ELISE. I don't think I should.

SCOTT. It's up to you.

> (**ELISE** *tentatively takes the receiver and holds it up to her ear.*)

ELISE. Hello?

> (*Brilliant light shines down on* **ELISE** *and the rest of the lights dim a bit. Everything is quiet except the storm that continues to rage outside. We can't hear what's being said, but someone is talking to her. This sequence takes as long as it needs to...*)

No no, I know you're not the one that caused the flooding this time.

> (**ELISE** *gasps.*)
>
> (*Then* **ELISE** *covers her mouth in shock.*)
>
> (*Then she grips the receiver tightly, bad news.*)
>
> (*Then she begins to cry.*)

It's just such a shame is all.

> (*Then she smiles with understanding through the tears.*)
>
> (*Then she smiles more and nods her head "yes" a few times.*)

Yes, I suppose we did have lots of chances to fix it.

> (*Then she nods her head "yes" again a few times.*)
>
> (*Then she looks over at* **SCOTT** *for a moment.*)

Yes, he does need rain boots. I told him.

> (*Then she laughs through her tears of joy.*)

(Then she hangs up the phone.)

*(Everyone's looking at **ELISE** as the lights restore. She's wiping away her tears. **LAVERNE** takes **ELISE**'s hand. She looks at her and nods.)*

LAVERNE. Elise? Are you okay?

*(**ELISE** hesitates, then stands up and clutches the phone to her chest.)*

ELISE. All right. All right, we made this mess and no one's coming to help. If we're going to survive, we'll have to do it ourselves. Let's build a boat.

End of Play

Vacuum

VACUUM was created for The 24 Hour Plays Viral Monologues (Artistic Director, Mark Armstrong). It premiered in Round 29 on June 15, 2021. The cast was as follows:

JILL . . . . Merle Dandridge

CHARACTERS

JILL

*(**JILL** starts a video camera. Wait, is it recording? Good. She steps back and the first thing that jumps out is her outfit: black silk pajamas with feathers. It's over the top. She checks herself in a mirror. She seems anxious, despite the outfit. She's in her living room.)*

JILL. Eh hm. I should, all right, I should start by saying that I don't date a lot. I want to date. Obviously, I'm doing this because I want to date. And other people want to date me. Just to be clear. I just...

I just find other people to be disappointing. Across the board disappointing, but specifically, in my experience, they are disappointing in terms of "romance." Not you, I'm not talking about you. Honestly, and I know we're not supposed to be this honest. Really, I'm the one who is disappointing in terms of romance. And then I end up taking it out my date because I just want everything to be perfect. And before you say it, I know there's nothing wrong with high standards.

(She sings a bit of an older showtune about falling in love.* It's abrupt, kind of like a defense mechanism. She's nervous, but she won't show it.)

You're looking at my outfit, right? These are my glamorous pajamas. Well, they're how I imagine glamorous women in the 1940s lounged around the

---

* A license to produce *Vacuum* does not include a performance license for any third-party or copyrighted music. Licensees should create an original composition or use music in the public domain. For further information, please see the Music and Third-Party Materials Use Note on page iii.

house. But before you start thinking of me as out of reach or champagne and bon bons all day or something, do you know what I was doing right before I started recording this?

> *(She holds up a finger to wait.)*
>
> *(Then she reaches offscreen...)*
>
> *(But she can't get whatever she's reaching for.)*
>
> *(So she gets up and gets...a Dyson vacuum cleaner.*)*

I was doing this.

> *(She starts to vacuum in her silk and feather pajamas and probably heels. It's the whole show. She talks over the vacuum...)*

Who does this? Honestly, who does this?

> *(She stops the vacuum.)*

That's ridiculous that I just did that. Why did I do that? I'm so uncomfortable. Eh hm. All right, that's my, that is my opening gambit. I hope you can sympathize. Oh, also my name is Jill. I'm Jill. Jesus, this is a horrible first impression.

You could have just said, "Hey, I'm Jill." Fuck. Should I start over?

> *(She sings a bit of the older showtune about falling in love. Okay, it's nice but now we're getting it's a nervous tick.)*

Okay, just... Hey, I'm Jill. I am a librarian, I love listening to true crime podcasts, I had a really beautiful

---

* A license to produce *Vacuum* does not include a license to publicly display any branded logos or trademarked images. Licensees must acquire rights for any logos and/or images or create their own.

goldfish until recently, but I don't dwell on sad things, and I usually find a way to fuck up romance, but not this time. I'm admitting that I'm terrible with dating and relationships and managing my fears up front so you can see how this time will be different. And my friend Brenda told me this would be good for my self-esteem. But it doesn't feel good for my self-esteem right now.

Why did I do this?

Why did I do this?

Fucking Brenda.

> *(She looks like she might cry. But she doesn't. She quickly wipes the tears away from her eyes and exhales into a smile. And then sings a bit of the older showtune about falling in love. But this time it's quietly to herself. It's short and she quickly shakes it off.)*

Look, if you made it this far, what's wrong with you? No, I'm kidding. I do that. I'm just not very good at... Eh hm, if you made it this far, maybe we can disappoint each other or, fuck, just completely ruin the idea of romance for each other. High standards. But while we're doing that damage...we won't be alone.

> *(She reaches to turn the camera off. Once it's done, she stands alone. Then...)*

I probably should have kept the vacuum on.

End of Play

www.ingramcontent.com/pod-product-compliance
Lightning Source LLC
Chambersburg PA
CBHW051438290426
44109CB00016B/1602